Content

Volume 97:2 Summer 2007

Poems

Centrefold

Reviews

Endpapers

POEMS

❧

... the surface of the sea folding
over events as they unfold as if nothing happened.
—*Ian Davidson*

Andrea Dow
Semele

All she wanted was everything
his wife had: him naked,
fierce as Hades on her skin,
his heart a warring drum, his breath
a heat-wave over Phlegethon.
How young she is, how eager
to be devastated. All on fire
to give her eyes, her limbs,
the unborn life within,
to have him once, the only way she can't
and burn.

Peter Porter

The Castaway Is Washed Ashore

She was the ship I sailed in, or
    We twinned as just one ship,
A Mother and a Son, assured
    Of one another's grip.
We guessed it wouldn't be for life,
A boy becalmed, a seasoned wife.

Whatever, there would come the storm,
    The light propitious fade;
Suburban living was the norm,
    A slovenly parade.
Which one would fall, which doomed to drown,
If climbing up were settling down?

The storm would blow us separately –
    For her, poor doctoring,
Stifled in her own blood's sea,
    I, at her skirts to cling.
Then Education's sad voice hit
My ears and I joined mine to it.

Out on the selfish ocean tossed,
    The storm now just a squall,
Apocalypse the only Cross
    At all empirical:
My *placement* was below the salt,
A setting? Or a Primal Fault?

A second ship – this was another
        Woman marked to die.
No strong resemblance to my Mother,
        But, like her, serving my
Absurd disintegration, taking
Her need beyond a quick forsaking.

Mixed metaphors sail on apace,
        The ship goes down and then
A second time the splintered face,
        A Castaway again –
A pair of ragged claws might row
Me safely from the undertow.

Quotations like a flag unfurled
        In cruel convenience
Showed my position in the world,
        The past my present tense.
As mushrooms, rose the childish faces,
A succulence of desert places.

As if in time's conjunctions, I
        Flew past the sugared peaks
Of Greenland – portholes bled the sky
        For Frequent Flyer geeks –
Life had to make its proffered run
Between extinction and the sun.

Such was the beach I scrambled up,
        Like Crusoe seeming saved,
The storm still simmered in its cup
        Which through my dreams had raved.
The mind, that navigating hand,
Now sought to drown me on the land.

John Burnside
An Essay Concerning Solitude

*And your solitude will bear immense fruit in
the souls of men you will never see on earth.*
– Thomas Merton

1 Our Marital Selves

Like something that runs
forever beyond our keeping,
this silent movie on the LCD
unspools, while we go on with something else;

no bells to toll, no promises to keep,
their candlelight, and summers at the lake,
stacked in a cupboard, golden, or solid white
in that yellowish glow we choose to mistake
for knowledge;

        how they walk home in the snow
and stand at the kitchen table, ignoring the phone,
remembering minus or π
in the milk of a textbook;

how, every night, the house is folded up
and put away;

        and how, in the foregone conclusion
of ache, or departure,
they never look back, although they are grateful
for this
      like the life neverending:

one thing for sure in a future they cannot dismantle,
barley fields blurring to stone, then the silver of autumn,
bones in the bridal dress, fragments of shell in the icing.

2 Women In Photographs

Because they know exactly what to do,
scrubbing a table down, or wrapping a corpse
in coal-tar and Sunday best;
                                    because they wait
so perfectly, in sculleries that smell
of bleached sheets, or the memory of liver,

they seem the private versions of a life
we thought of years ago, but set aside
for later: quiet, L-shaped narratives
of washrooms, and the hum of terminus
that waits all afternoon to be admitted;

women with empty faces, pocked with light,
girls in their later years, their dreams of harvest
folded and put away in attic rooms

with vanished children, trinkets, windfall plums
and long-dead husbands, cleansed, then laid to rest,
like innocents, before the staggered dark.

3 Amour De Soi

Like saying a thing, then knowing it is true,
this private love, that smoothing out the lines
of self-regard;
                flowers or rain in the mirror, the windows
filling with the blaze of early spring

and, all the time, that absence in the glass
coming to life as gaze, or the near recognition
that keeps the soul on track;

how, sometimes, going out,
you meet yourself coming in
from a different weather,

rain on your sleeves, or the white of japonica
lighting your face, when you turn and the shadows are what
they ought to be – no black, and no hidden caesura,

even if what you see has the transitive air
of something already known: not the fog of possession
but everything given up, or revised, or forgotten
to live *in* the present, not *for*, and the moment unending.

4 The Turing Test

I could have wakened
in a house like this,
hearing the wind arrive
at a turn in the stairs,

rabbits, there, or
something like a badger,
owls in the slur
from one thought to the next;

buzzard-light, rat-light,
skewed across a wall,
whole families of muntjac
stopping to prove
the absolute of snow
against a door;

witch-hazel, meadow,
raptures of fox in a passing
headlamp
as it drifts across the floor

and, somewhere behind it all,
suggested, *sub voce*,
the animal
that I might still become

if I walked to the end
of the hallway and entered
the one room of nothing but grasses:
timothy, fescue, quaking grass, silky agrostis,
feathering into the light
like the thought of forever.

5 Bethany

Waking at 3 a.m. is becoming an art;
an art, or a gift, delivered through sleep and quiet,

parcels of snow and sky
from another country,

lights from a childhood that feels
so recent, we might not have aged at all.

Give us this day, we say, and continue
moving the pieces, trying to puzzle it out,

a picture of fog, or stars, through an open window,
hares in the long grass, mice in the folds of the yard,

the wisp of sun unfurling from a wall
that matches us

for warmth and transience,
the fabric of a life, asleep and waking,

finding and losing its way
in the house of the echo.

6 On The Border

For afterlife, I'll wake in a motel
near Ajo, in some inexpensive room
with furniture that looks like *trompe l'oeil*,

the smell of the desert, cholla and creosote,
trapped in the clothes I have folded across a chair,
the TV like a mute child by the door

waiting to see what will happen when the wind
unfolds through the room like the angel of the lord
in a *quattrocento* painting: citrus and leaf-green

traces in the shape I take for wings
and enter, as if discovered, or silently claimed

by the grammar of morning,
the yellow, unspeakable Word.

Medbh McGuckian

How Despair May Be Transformed Into A Diamond

As payment for your colour storm
An acid sky blackens every flower.
You feel your breath touching down
And hold on to the voice you know
On each lip corner, two now frozen
Hedges to your country.

You can still alight on words
Or sharpen them as you wish;
You can linger on and stretch them
Like the skin of a birch bark letter
Read before a mirror.
How easily you get what you want.

But if you step on the spot
The fully-grown mouth passes
The feather of a red-headed
Irish angel three times between you.
When you are breath-bound
It is purely breath that is stopped.

Tavoletta

Before the snow of the city
Too soon after Christmas
Had three times melted
Under the tenderest sewing clouds,

All that was audible in the world
Was the last island in motion
Cascading like a slanting plate
Or a discarded crinoline

In the buckled roof of the rain.
The mind does not know
It is counting caustic sands
Rushed from solid rock.

*

The picture hanging over my stove
Gradually deepens its bone brown
To a holding back of colour without end
Such as prevails at dawn:

To older colours where rose
Bleaches out and blue suffers,
Dark violet bricks in feathers
On the weather side of a wall:

An airwell on the left wing –
Golden crucifixion through which he slept –
Which is enough protection in itself,
But emptier than the parish church...

David Morley
Sèsi O Lety U Písku[1]

I have come a long way and am almost there.
'You were almost there except for this frontier.'
I approach the frontier and see the wire.
'You passed me without looking but I was still present.'
I am almost there except for this frontier.
'There was nothing to stop you yet you rode back to the city.'
You pass me without looking but I am still present.
'Except for the wire there was nothing to stop you.'
There is nothing to stop me yet I ride back to the city.
'You made the brass boast you stopped for one night.'
Except for the wire there is nothing to stop me.
'And you saw this wire. It made you exceptional.'
I make the brass boast I'll stop there one night.
'It made you exceptional. Apart from the others.'
I see the wire. It makes me exceptional.
'Apart from the others, who stared back through the wire.'
It makes me exceptional: apart from the others.
'And you approached the frontier. And saw the wire.'
A part of the others. They stare back through the wire:
You came a long way. You are almost there.

1. *Sèsi*: A Voice (Romani); *Lety U Písku*: Nazi concentration camp for Roma from Bohemia, responsible for the eradication of more than half of the Roma population in the Czech lands. The Czech population often supported the extermination, especially members of the Protectorate police force. It is the site, today, of a factory farm for 13,000 pigs.

Ruth Padel
Mother Of Pearl

Come in, signor. Quickly. Let me show you round.
Bend, please – the gate is four foot three.
  We call it The Door of Humility.
You can interpret this in many ways. Some say
this little entry, such a mighty structure,

speaks to us today of hope, of other bad times
the church survived. So – take your breath.
  We're safe now, friend. Touch the inside wall
   and you have at your fingers' end
the start of the Church Herself. The basilica you see
was built by Emperor Justinian, sixth century AD.

But under is church of Constantine – consecrated in 325
to Maria Theotokos. We honour Mary-Giving-Birth-
  to-God. Not the Madonna with her Child
   though her lily's our native flower. You're free, monsieur.
You can go to limesinks of the north and find
it blooming now. White hands of leathery velvet. Moony, wild.

Stand here, in nave, I'll lift a hatch. There – see caramel
snakeskin glimmer, lower floor? That's mosaic, cut
  for Constantine in 324. Like carpet, isn't it? Our Church
   is built on that. Mortar shells last week broke many... here –
but these tesserae, wine-dark waves in parallel,
amber geometries of seventeen hundred years, survive.

The church above is fortified like praying heart.
Like castle, this is true. Seigneur, it had to be. You see
  what's happening now. Asylum is safe place (step here,
   round citizens) but Justinian knew asylum's danger, too.
He built high walls round Bethlehem so church
could have wide doors. See the outline, triple-arched?

(Sorry the smell. Guns won't be breaking through.)
Welcoming, wouldn't they be – impressive, those big
   big doors? They were blocked in, smoodged
   up in Ottoman years so Turkish giaours
couldn't gallop in on war stallions, full fig.
Did you bring water? Medicine? Food?

Well... come among the rows – a forest, isn't it? –
of shadow-columns. Run your fingers down them.
  Local sandstone, khaki-ginger, quarried from our hills
  where fruit trees of the Bible are (must be) in bloom.
Pomegranate blossom, scarlet fizz against gloss leaves.
Mulberry, almond, purple cream of Judas trees

in flower just this season, when he hung himself.
See the flicker, when I open door a crack? Or
  that brachiating goldfish shimmer, over shelf
  of Corinth-petal capital, every pillar? They'd glisten
like moonrise if we lit the hanging lamps between.
Have you seen mother-of-pearl on column-heads before?

Our town is famous, sir, for mother-of-pearl.
We understand its vulnerability. How to incise curls
  on brittle mucus cloud without it breaking. Other time,
  I take you to my brother's shop, down steep crusader stairs
behind the church. We sell drop-earrings like milk air.
Translucent buttons, carved like roses, carved like birds.

In the Bible, it's a stable where He's born. Round here they say
it was a cave. Take my hand for steps to crypt. Let me go first.
  Dark, narrow, yes, but Greek Orthodox run this part –
  even now, there'll be a candle. In 135, Emperor Hadrian
made this cave sacred to pagan god, Adonis. It became
criminal act for Christians, telling stories of rebirth.

Dictator's nightmare, isn't it, signor – you write it,
in your paper – the appeal of vulnerability?
 So – the Manger! Touch, that's OK. Like Helena,
 Roman Empress – she crept here, scooped her hand
in wall of living rock and found a secret basin
made of clay. Her son built his basilica above.

They were late-comers to our faith. The Bible says
it's never too late to remake who you are. To reconsider.
 In next cave, here, Saint Jerome worked Bible into Latin.
 Next cave, these too-short tombs commemorate
the Innocents. King Herod told soldiers to exterminate
little sons of Bethlehem. Did you see *Schindler's List*?

That guy on horse above some town, watching men
enter ghetto, bayonet doors, drag children
 out of wardrobes, out from under beds?
 That happened here also – in Manger Square
where you came in. All the mothers of Bethlehem
one by one, their mouths torn open, screaming for their sons.

In this cave, the One that got away was born.
But real stuff's covered. You can't see... Helena
 sleeved the clay manger in silver. Justinian
 plastered marble on these walls, roof, floor.
You like this outer curtain round the manger,
orange-flame brocade? My mother stitched the fringe.

The inner curtain, sky-blue silk like cupola of heaven
with racy-lacy angels, came from the Isle of Cos.
 But the spot beneath, my friend (I may say,
 "friend"?), is where He first touched earth.
In 1717, they cut this silver star in floor below,
with fourteen flaming points. Marble's stained

where cracks round screws have let in water.
Looks like waving starfish, tamped into the marble,
    flat-lit from above by fourteen silver lamps
    to represent communities all over world
who worship here. For our church is sustained
by every heart upon the planet. Even in Africa.

That's why you've come sir, isn't it? Millions dream
these altars, facing across the cave. Altar of the Manger –
    and Altar of the Magi, look, behind. Wise Men
    from the East stood here before Him in their starry,
complicated robes, where you're standing now.
Have you seen Shepherds' Field, outside the town?

That's where the sky lit up. Christmas cards in West
provide you snow, running deer, green shards of fir
    and holly. I have seen. But it happened here,
    with twisted-toffee gnarls of olive trees, shining
in angel glow. And *our* flowers dormant in the ground –
sparrow-wort, broomrape and Yeruham iris, logo

of Society for Protection (I belong) of Nature.
In our shop we sell, also, figures carved in olive wood.
    Three different kings. A donkey, ox and camel,
    very beautiful. A shepherd boy, carrying justborn
lamb on back, running to tell about the angel.
The church is part of Bethlehem. Convents cluster near

like satellite snowdrop bulbs around original.
They say it looks in air like ivory
    carved from a single tusk. Our town must be
    most captured, most destroyed, in history.
Persians sacked, in 614, but left the church alone.
They saw the Wise Men's clothes on Byzantine mosaic –

they recognized the holiness. In 634
Arabs captured church; made shrine for Muslim prayer.
    In 747, the town was dust again. In earthquake –
    but sir, the same thing happened. Church remained
unharmed. In eleventh century, with Crusaders in the West,
was feeling against Christians here. Of course there was.

But Al-Hakim didn't danger church because of Muslim
shrine. Everything played its part. Before Western invasion,
    capture of Jerusalem, Tancredi rode to Bethlehem
    with Baldwin of le Bourg. They took our church
(we've seen a lot of "taking", sir) in 1099. Baldwin
was crowned Christmas Day 1101, First High Crusader King.

In 1187, his kingdom came to end. Nothing here lasts long
that's from outside. The Latins left. But in 1192,
    Salah al-Din allowed priests back to tend
    the altar. Khwarizmian Turks took the town
in 1244, but left basilica alone... Am I boring you?
Each time, so far, our white small town

was crushed to powder-stone, the church survived.
That's all I meant to say. Everyone's let it be.
    Yet it looked, by 1350, as you see it now –
    a citadel. All the West, all Christendom
gave money to protect. To fortify. Philip of Burgundy
gave pinewood, Edward IV sent roofing lead

from England. We'll get help from America, you'll see,
any day. Is Christian land. We have two hundred citizens here
    who fled inside. No food.... You're leaving, sir? If you think
    my voice is wrong, I'm not myself today. I would have
taken you to the garden shown you flowers of the Bible
that belongs to everyone. Blue alkanet, white asphodel...

This is your story, too. I thought you were a friend.
What happens to the man who has betrayed
 his moral anchor or its earthly image, glances at the crafts
 of holiness, then looks away? Bend, please. Take care –
they've mounted cranes around the church, with snipers
Maybe you know them; and they know you.

Other time, if you come back, it may be all you see
is tinsel among rubble, mother-of-pearl
 dust, heaven rolled back
 like bolt of mourning cloth on a market stall –
and under, all the darnels of the Bible. Spiny zilla,
holy thistle, Syrian acanthus, grey nightshade, Christ Thorn.

Church of the Nativity, Bethlehem, Easter 2002

Neetha Kunaratnam
The Afterlife

After every war
someone has to clean up. Things won't
straighten themselves, after all.
  — Szymborska, *The End and the Beginning*

And someone will have to clean up,
But this is no job for ordinary Joes,
Only specialists padded in moon boots,
Facemasks, and white chemical suits,

So someone will have to write out a cheque
For the foreign input, the expertise
And expensive equipment:
The mine detectors and nerve sensors,

Somebody will need to order them
From the front of the catalogue, ignore
The new solar-powered, GPS models, plump
For the standard, remote-controlled breed,

As faithful and expendable as *someone else*,
Sought to cordon off the area, skirt the perimeters
On tiptoe, and mark out the dimensions
Of the operation with only sniffer dogs in tow.

Someone will need to believe the aggrieved can
Make a difference, pray in numbers, and petition
Our leaders to subsidize the farmers, who can no
Longer reap lest they're blown into thin air...

Someone will have to locate then collect
Any bright packages dropped in the interim,
Since the bombers droned off into the night,
Their black boxes still replaying screams,

And someone sort out the dried food
From the prosthetic limbs, filter out the notes
Of explanation, and decipher a rationale
From the mistakes made in translation.

Someone will have to point out
That mustard leaves might not survive the blasts,
And checking they've turned red might set off
A barrage of blinding and a cluster of regrets,

Somebody will have to teach the children
That these M&Ms aren't filled with peanuts
But pack a mighty punch. Explain that
A bomb as small as a battery can turn a sheep into a cloud

Jean Sprackland
Thaw

From the helicopter he sees at last
anomalies in the pattern of melt.
The snow has turned informer.

It must have seemed the perfect accomplice,
erasing everything, the way a quilt
might be thrown over a wrecked bed.

Earth was another – tons of it,
shovelled by hand and then by machine,
a loan from the building site
where somebody's cousin worked –

and time, of course. The wound
closed, scabbed over. In summer
there were rough grass, yellow flowers,
even butterflies.

Circle again, he says, and hears
his own voice cracking and slipping.
He reads the diagram of broken snow.
He'll need to radio down, get it ground-truthed.
They'll peel back the scab,
expose what everyone knows already:

under the heaviest winter, the stash of warmth.

J.P. Nosbaum
Hiroshige Misremembered

How the snow is its focus in being not there.
How the world is its outline. How its absence weighs limbs
and branches down as white as paper, as the paper
is white.
        An old woman, back curved
beneath a parcel, head turned deep
into the print, rests on a cane or
slip of stick and stares at the same drifts
of nothing as we, drawing her out
to share with us these cool halls
of glass displays and shoe sole whispers,
as she draws us out of all
perspective through the glass and into the snow:
an atmosphere of pure silence falling on our ears.

Linda Chase
Sometimes Snow

Sometimes snow lights up all the drowsy fields
at night like cool electric blankets spread
beneath the moon, reflecting what the moon
reflects without a thank you to the sun,
no nod of gratitude, since light is light,
night is night, allowing you to see the dark
and through it to the light of snow, how dark
dying into day, tries to keep light
before a fading thaw reminds the sun
it's indebted to an impartial moon
for offering a surface so blank, spread
out so thin, so willing across those fields.

Last night you went to Shropshire on the train
and saw everything. Darling, don't explain.

Ian Davidson
Skulte And Saulkrasti

on the train line north of Riga. a line of
sand dunes topped with scots pine, birch and
rowan and a grey Baltic whipped into small
waves. what the fisherman in their small
inflatables saw as they stood around with their
backs to the wind much longer than was necessary
to discuss their catch. the left hand uncertain
as to what the right was doing
and just beyond their line of vision.
the next day thunder
rumbled in the background, rolling around the city,
the climate out of control
the heating boiler set to zero a heavy shower

forecast and all for nothing. we were wet, dripping,
leaking through the boundaries hands breaking
through the surface of the sea cross hatched
and a line of waves breaking along the
shore. my back was a windbreak to fine
sand whipped up by a stiff breeze and a face
turned upward to a grey sky and a trawler turning to
show its length and the surface of the sea folding
over events as they unfold as if nothing happened

Tomaž Šalamun
The Man I Respected

When I returned from Mexico, I looked like
death. My mouth collapsed
and disintegrated. I was paying a penalty
for my sins, my palate had dissolved.
I could touch my brain with my tongue.
It was painful, horrible and sweet.
While Svetozar sat outside in the waiting room,
I tore down the instrument case.
No, I am not being precise, he left the office
before me, I only suspected who he was, I didn't even
know him. When I sat in the chair,
my energy tore down the instrument case.
To pass from world to world
means an earthquake. Yesterday he died.

Scarlet Toga

Overnight snowfall filled everything.
The pools are emeralds.
I talked to people
with noble mouths.

They brought cymbals and bronze,
a chafer wrapped in stiff paper,
they swung it in a handcart and sang,
we heard how the fortresses were knocked down.
The dust from the ruins is still damp.

We burned down and built from
the shit of camels and cows.
Yesterday on Elizabeth Street I saw
a man who had such a hat.

At Starbuck's it truly smells
of the roasteries of Trieste, the aroma
that they first carried away to Seattle.
We were still talking about two

supermodels (about cow dung),
hairstyles, little braids, goggles,
about the carefully outworn,
and I injected into myself
this text in the photo:

Jorge Vegas, soft shadow friend
whisper fire. Caress the blood
within. Set free the Buddha
cat in me, into ginger
haven, sugar stone smile...

Translated by Brian Henry

Claire Malroux
Grottoes

I

Without knowing us the dog rushes to greet us
from the path at the morning's most luscious moment when the sky
leans on the church's slate roof

Imperiously she leads us to the enchanted spots
of her dog's life

We must roll with here in the fields sniff the horse-pads
shake ourselves off in the stream which erases time's borders
like animal tracks

A bridge to our human joy so close
to her domain
and necessary to her happiness
as if a hint of eternity guided her by its smell

When we retrace our steps she'll hurl herself on us again
with grand gestures of gratitude

Swallows have no such fraternities
Barely curious, the horses will have turned away to cratch themselves
and embrace, cheek to cheek

Echo of the group gathered on a rocky promontory by the ancestor's eye
not so long ago at the heart of the grotto

II

At the grotto's mouth she forgot the spring
the grass's whispers the stridences the shiver and thunder
of the branches

shook off the sun's weight to penetrate its silence

Now she is no more than an arm of shadow a snake's sloughed skin
in the stone

Men have crawled into her body with torches
and flints

Europa Eurydice Persephone Beatrice

Their drawings destroy and beget themselves
horse's belly bison's hump and mammoth's chest
doe's head in a crotch

One reads: the god is closest to me in my enemy
With my sharpened lump of clay I hold him in my power
I am embodied in him
Or: you who pass by here help me to escape the stone trap

Some unique artist has left a signature: human
slender, sexless, future pastor of the catacombs

Another, is it the same, big-buttocked female carrying
her clitoris in front of her like a Perigourdine her bag
when she goes to market on the village square
at the hour when the sun gnaws the last bones of snow

III

Alone in her grotto where nothing except a rarer air asks questions

The branches up there grinding the dead on their way to a cloud-eden

Rarer matter than dew on a rose, shadow on a wall, the shiver
of skin stretched over the chasm

For the hermit the days' exhalations the leaves' prodigality the greenness of rain

What is a day after so many days?

A stone (sometimes white), a marker placed graciously but without indulgence on
path

Oh mask the dusks, fire off huge bouquets of dawns

Let your afternoons play at rolling down the slopes
as yesterday you slid your days on the shaft of the abacus
back and forth, without counting them

Where today they are impaled one by one in slow torture

Translated by Marilyn Hacker

Pascale Petit
The Treekeeper's Tale

I have set up house in the hollow trunk of a giant redwood.
My bed is a mat of pine needles. Cones drop their spirals

on my face as I sleep. I have the usual flying dreams.
But all I know when I wake is that this bark is my vessel

as I hurtle through space. Once, I was rocked in a cradle
carved from a coast redwood, its lullabies were my coracle.

I searched for that singing grove and became its guardian.
There are days when the wind plays each tree

like a new instrument in the forest-orchestra.
On wild nights mine is a flute. After years of solitude

I have started to hear its song. I lie staring at the stars
until the growth rings enclose me in hoops –

choirs of concentric colours, as if my tree is remembering
the music of the spheres. And I almost remember speaking

my first word, how it flew out of my mouth like a dove.
I have forgotten how another of my kind sounds.

John F. Deane
The Jesus Bones

It was full summer and the skylarks soared
over the wild meadow;
across ditch and hedgerow the dogrose
was draping its pink-rose shawl while the flowering brambles reached

dangerous fingers
towards the flowerbeds. A bat lay dead on the garage
window-ledge, amongst webs
and husks; it was curled up tight, perfect as a babyfist

though flies already
had laid their eggs in the sacred caverns of the ears;
I touched the fur and brushed the unresisting skin of night.
The holly leaves hymned in the sun

and small birds flitted through it;
it was shaping in torsion – all of us subject to corruption – a green
promise of clusters of the most scarlet of all berries; tree, I imagined,
of the knowledge of good and evil, its bitter roots

driving into the humus of our sleep. I would be, at times,
animal, thread of the skein
of earth, free of the need of redemption. Once I crept along a ditchtop,
in a tunnel of rhododendron, on earth mould,

leaf mould, on blossom-droppings, the tiny hardnesses
stippling palms, and knees;
this was everyday adventure,
the eyes of blackbirds following and their alarm calls,

with the strange and beetly
insects frighening me, their throbbing, their pebble-eyes.
I could fall silent there, hidden on the pulsebeat of the earth, mind
vacant, body stilled. Part of it. To receive.

And watched the fox slip by the drain outside,
there, uncareful, in daylight,
each russet hair sun-burnished, the breathfilled brush
like an old guardianship, a queen's train, that sorrowing eye

rounded, where a moon-sliver shape of white
startled me; her long tongue lolling, the teeth were visible
in a grim fox-smile. My breathing stopped and a tiny shiver of fellowship
touched my spine. A moment, merely. Then

she was gone. A magpie
smattered noisily in the trees: *one for gloria, for hosanna*. If, in our waking,
we could mould it all into a shape, beautiful and at peace
the way the electrically burnt heart of Jesus

found rest in the rock tomb
though we are many, seam and femur, root-system,
belly, spleen. Night, and the moon dressed the storm-black clouds
in scarves of buttermilk-white while a solitary star, as if hesitating, sat

over the eucalyptus tree. We –
not animal enough and cruel beyond thought –
go scattering blood over the earth
as we might scatter water off our fingers,

big-headed man, articulate, stitching and unstitching
mindlessly as we pass. The Jesus bones
have been nailed into the timber of the tree, the blood
in its revolutions

pouring through the puncture-holes, this man,
of localised importance, this Jesus-fox, who broiled fine fish
on a nest of stones by the lakeshore; this
rag-and-bone man, this stranger, this lover, giver, priest.

Tim Liardet
Ur-blue

The last time I saw my father he had
the eyes of an angel. I do not say this sentimentally,
or in false hope, or even to imply I knew

before then what the eyes of an angel would
or would not be. But at least because his body seemed
as if it had recently come through the flames,

had walked through flames which changed the look of him
when his skin grew tighter as if it were burned;
because he brought up the wasted scarp of his knee

towards his chin in a jack-knifing movement
and tried yet again to pull off his pyjamas
as if this might seem a normal thing to do –

his eyes were either the eyes of an angel
or did not quite belong to his body any more
as if he had somehow become another species

*

and was already no longer my father.
                            Do you think you know blue?
The colour for which so many remote
and Neolithic tribes have no word. His eyes were the source

of blue, where light discovered it, where blue sprung;
they were lapis lazuli – lit from behind;
they were gentian and cyanosis, sapphire and lavandula

bidding for the crush of molecules;
they were Prussian blue and cerulean, cobalt and smalt,
they were indigo and woad – they were all of these

and none of them, they were blue, more than blue;
and his pupils edged across like the soul's eclipse
and the blue around them bred in the way

that took it out of colour into something else.
His radiocative body from which the pounds
had fallen away like so much clothing took the blue

and made it otherworldly at its own expense.
He looked through me then, as if I was
a newly cleaned window on the route he was taking.

He looks through me now.

Jane Duran
Tuna

My feet entering this mountain river
        go white and numb.
    I wear the white socks of numbness.

    They are like an event.
When I reach for the cactus fruit – *tuna*,
        it releases tiny hair-like thorns
    into the palm of my hand.

I search for them now. Sometimes
    I hold my hand up
        to the pale blue sky to find them.

I open the ochre of the *tuna* and I am alive,
    its seeds run through me.

Now my arms in the river are numb, my body
    like those Aymara weavings, the dyes circulating
        then stilled, all those feelings I will ever feel

mapped out. What is happening to my feet, my hands?
    My feet and my hands can just touch
        the two ends of Chile –

I lie north to south in it, I am as slim
    as good fortune, as the man who has walked
        all the way here, over the mountains.

I meet its fleeting rigour
    with numbness and a variable pain.

Anne Stevenson
Before Eden

for Paul Stangroom

A day opens, a day closes,
Each day like every other day.
No day is like another day.

A wave crashes, a wave caresses,
Each wave like the next wave.
None sweeps the same arc on the sand.

A wall fits its belt to a hill
As a mason fits stone to hand.
No stone's like any other stone.

And every stone has a like stone.
Why should another spring surprise me?
The gorse still erupts from the scrubland.

The gulls again screech to the landfill.
What claims identity
That isn't self-propelled, vicious, multiple, alone?

Think of how it was before Eden.
God held his breath,
The fresh-moulded clay in his hands,

Hesitating between dream and achievement.
The mountains were there,
Fixed in a clear, viscous element

He would need to exchange for air.
Trees flowered, gorgeous as palaces,
All without fruit, without rot.

Had bacteria and seeds been invented?
Yes, but they didn't have uses.
The birds and creatures were there

Evolved already in his mind,
Lifelessly waiting while
The pivotal question tormented him:

What sort of nature did he want?
Once he'd breathed life into Adam,
He knew he couldn't take it back.

He himself would have to be
Re-created, risking
His hand-made system, risking death.

No life without birth.
No growth without waste.
No first step without a last.

It was such perfect weather,
That sparkling morning of the sixth day
When God, in his pride, looked over

His hard week's work, saw that it was good,
And hesitated.
If the sky had admitted one cloud,

If the mountains had understood
Their whispering ice
Or loved the molten nature of being,

If a bird had cried out, or if
A locust had filleted sound,
Or if terror had *said*...

He might have thought the fifth day would suffice.
But the *Gipfel* nursing the rhododendrons,
Even the Tree of Knowledge, said nothing.

It was the silence broke him in the end.
With every perfect day identical,
No animating evil could arise.

So God bent down and sighed the words
"I will."
He spoke, and Adam opened all his eyes.

Weekend Courses at Stones Barn

Set in the rural Borders, Stones Barn is an idyllic setting for these new courses:

14–16 Sept 07 *The Music of what Happens* – John Burnside and Fiona Sampson
A weekend exploring ways of telling stories in poetry and lyrics, ranging from the border ballads to the current crop of singer-songwriters. There will be time to work on your own and one to one with the tutors.

16–18 Nov 07 *Guiding Spirits* – Mimi Khalvati
In this course, we will look at the work of poets who have invoked a guiding spirit, who converse with its presence or absence, and whose vision borrows light from a star that never grows cold. We will read inspirational texts, write in the light of that reading, and see what happens when we do.

4–6 Apr 08 *Ecopoetry and the Natural World* – David Morley
Natural phenomena may 'centre and stake the imagination' (Seamus Heaney), but natural selection reveals to us unstable versions as well as subversions of life – much as a poet drafts metaphors for reality. Workshops, field trips, and discussions over this enjoyable weekend in Lakeland.

30 May – 1 Jun 08 *The Sense of Sound* – Don Paterson (weekend course)
Don Paterson will focus on the music of poetry, and how poets manipulate sound – to intensify their meaning, make poems more memorable and construct the engine of poetic composition. General principles; advanced techniques of rhyme and sound-patterning.

Fees: £170 (for each course)
Local accommodation, very reasonably priced. A list of B&Bs may be downloaded from the website, or phone for details.

Bookings: Maddy Prior, Stones Barn, Roweltown, Carlisle, Cumbria, CA6 6LA
    01697 748 424   sbadmin@maddyprior.co.uk   www.maddyprior.co.uk

Conor O'Callaghan
The Pilot Light

Every night the spare cylinder's yellow
has shone in the bathroom window
like one of those lop-sided moons
dangling out over Clare,
that stray's bray carried thirty Augusts
and the island's intermittent pinhead
run aground on day.
There have been afternoons
when the white manes flattened
and even the cement out front
was warm underfoot.
I'm leaving the gate stoned back,
the pilot light budding in your name.
Is it safe? Sure, and I like what it says.

The Armory Golf Range

is easily missed on the parkway
among biscuit joints and pre-owned auto traders.
You blast away from the city
towards pylons, wilderness.
It kills most latish Sunday blues.

Next door, from where it rents its title, is tidal:
high is waves of hardware in camouflage;
low is a deserted lot of red earth and mica.

Odd weeks Rick, your patron,
locks his flat screen flickering inside,
trusts you'll toss your bucket on his stoop when quits
and frequents a dive that trades
by the same handle two lots back.

Last man standing,
once you press against the chicken wire
with half a mind to ask the jeeps and tanks
and missile launchers where they get their balls.
Only there's seldom a soul home
and such irony, you do see, is beneath its calling.

Those you get are luminous.
Chipped through the vanishing point,
they bloom again within minutes:
mushrooms, planetarium spots,
a galaxy reachable on foot
some alien other than yourself will fetch.

Seán Ó Ríordáin
Apathy Is Out

There's not a fly, moth, bee,
man or woman created by God
whose welfare's not our responsibility;
to ignore their anxiety
isn't on.
There's not a mad man in Gleann na Gealt
we shouldn't sit with
and keep company, since
he's sick in the head
on our behalf.

There's not a place, stream or bush,
however remote; or a flagstone
north, south, east nor west
that we shouldn't consider
without affection and empathy.
No matter how far South Africa,
no matter how distant the moon,
they're part of us by right:
there's not a single spot anywhere
we're not a part of. We issue from everywhere.

Translated by Greg Delanty

Nick Laird
Terrain

Though we cannot detect them, infra-red rays from the system's
security sensors are scanning the rooms, and our surnames
are secret and neat in security ink on the back of the picture frames,

though readily fluorescent under ultra-violet light. In our own rainbow
of visibility, you'd been watching a property show and had dozed
and now the screen was frantic, driving home through snow, alone.

I read somewhere one-hundreth of that static is cosmic radiation
interfering from the very edge of space and time, some ninety billion
trillion miles away, from the word go, from the Big Bang.

Proponents of string theory posit twenty-six dimensions,
though we have the ability to pick up only four, with these senses
I can now detune – settled in beside your skin and warmth and sleep –

to some unnumbered octave, some unremembered reach,
where all the other universes press like lovers up against us.

Matthew Francis
Was

1

The wallpaper was a forest of fishbones.
The dressing-gown was a shroud against the door.
A given moment was marked off by headlamps.

It was still too early for any ghosts.
This area of night was inhabited.
A colourless woman was walking down the street.

The dark was dangling under the lamp-posts.
A settlement of moths was pitching its tents.
There was a consortium of trees, consorting.

The house was next to a dormant canal.
There was an extra blackness where the trees were.
The railway was shuttling lights to London.

2

It was expected that you would gallivant.
It was quite possible to pretend to play.
I was knocking my house down with a tennis ball.

A car was falling apart in a bamboo thicket.
I was picking up pages of book in the grass.
A house was tangled somewhere hereabouts.

The canal was so green you could ride on it.
The water was like Guinness with a green head.
Marsh gas was proddable out of it with a stick.

There was a hedged garden with silver birches.
I was shouted at there by a sudden woman.
It was hard work pretending to be a child.

3

My father was an artist in marzipan.
His egg-shaped head was visible through the crowds.
He was courtly, and called girls Miss in shops.

The war was still within range of anecdotes.
There was a hundred-pound sack of flour, and a rat...
He was cured of Gyppo guts by eating oranges.

His top speed was twenty-eight miles an hour.
The light in the shed was the colour of new wood.
He was failing to make the evenings into a boat.

He was fearless with puns and boiling sugar.
The table was a Cézanne of candied fruit.
An icing submarine was his masterpiece.

4

Morning was broken by my mother's singing.
There was a pigeon that sang one note five times.
The air was popping with rifle fire from Bisley.

The weather near the school was made of screams.
Outside was a grey area for jostling in.
Playtime was guarded by rhymes and stringy elastic.

Inside was an experiment in formica.
Maths was a jackstraws game of coloured rods.
The queasy smell of plasticine was on me.

The road home was clustered with enemies.
It was impossible to look burly while slinking.
I was practising the vowels that would make me tough.

5

This was when knees were worn in the open air.
The pavement was not your friend, nor was the winter.
When it snowed I was allowed to wear leggings.

Cabbage was cooked everywhere at once.
Curry was pacified in its circle of rice.
Wine was a sweet gold opened at Christmas.

The TV was afloat on a sea of fuzz.
It was switched on early to let it breathe.
The end of it was a diminishing star.

The typewriter was shaken by bouts of Xs.
Interference was more general in those days.
At night the radio was seized by foreigners.

6

There was a neighbour, high up in the city,
who was swinging on the banister of his office
when the whirlpool of the stairs was his nemesis.

There was a brown dog who ducked out of the leash
once too often, and was lost in an strange town
where there was a shouting man in every garden.

There was my father who lay with his eyes closed
on the floor as if he was looking at something
that was hurtling towards him from the inside.

And there was what passed for me at the time
who was left behind in the greens by the canal
but was there when I last looked, and still is.

Tom Lowenstein
Six Untitled Poems From A Longer Sequence

Between the dead hollyhocks and kitchen
window, a labyrinth cross-hatched
with this violin partita. Spiders' shambles.

*

Hornet squatting by an excavation in this small
scabby apple, grasps in front of it a large wet
half-fermented crumb and knowledgably munches.

*

A scum build-up at the hidden
sluice gate. Pressed into itself, the
water takes on a cast of the metal.

*

At last I can see the blue face of the
tractor that up beyond the Mill House
willows had sincerely laboured.

*

Bell-fade and the clock tocks onward.
Cold light on the flushwork. Past
and future: same wind on the ruins.

*

This was an old hedge I sheltered in
against a squall from the Atlantic. And grew
closer to the twigs and small dead foliage.

Stephen Knight
Where I Stand

You don't recall opening this door
to stand here, looking at the sky.
Tears in the curtain, toys on the floor,
a three-year-old as well. —Do I
belong to her? Does she know
who I am? (you ask yourself) or why
I place my forehead on the window
now and then? ...You do know this:
the world within your reach is so
remote it needs more emphasis,
more light to reach you where
you stand, tilted as if to kiss
the glass or else to say a prayer.
Behind you still, a three-year-old
colours mermaid scales and hair,
making of her hand a fist to hold
her paintbrush long enough to stain
the paper orange, pink and gold.
Stand here, looking at the rain.
Stopped in the land of either/or.
Smears on the window-pane.

Jane Holland
Flood At Boscastle

Ten steps down, through Sargasso weeds
green as the felt walls
of a fish tank, is a door
through which only haruspices may pass, bearded
and with credit cards,
to buy sacred books
and strange instruments for scrying
so they might peer inside
the living heart
and say which house survives,
which doesn't.

Portal invulnerable, they cry,
to the left-hand of the rising river,
thy charmed walls shall not be blowholes
for the unclenched well of the waters,
no *spiraculum mirabile*
breathing mud into the underworld.

Later, stripped to the waist, men dig
blackened books
from the whale ribs of a cottage,
then stamp up through mud
to the Cobweb
for a finger or two of whisky,
predicting more rain
on the print of a wetted thumb.

John Powell Ward
The Humanist's Creed

"First, to respect each other; humbly love
the offending or uncontrolled; aid the poor;
help out your mates and kin and easefully
use their help too; the human has this lot and love.
This tenet we owe the Christians and their grace.

Second however, to know we must and can
be self-sufficient; turn to no gods or myths
for tasks it's ours to make, to find and take;
here is the one road now, realise the earth
we see is largely ours; wholly ours to shape.

Third, seeing this human independence
as a self-searching, to pull the material
aim into the human; perceive ourselves, put
science's laboratory in house and park,
air flight and street; the world. Know and be known."

A calm and good and reasonable creed.
Calm and reasonable and good indeed.

Gregory Warren Wilson
Sleepless At Dawn

What comes to mind is the canary
brought up with nightingales
whose improvisations it learned to imitate
and knowing no other believed were its own.

Friedrich Hölderlin
Brevity

"Why are you so brief? Don't you love song any more
    As you did before? A young man in days of hope
        You sang without ever
            Finding an end to it."

My song is like my happiness. – Do you want to bathe
    Joyfully in sunset light? It has gone and earth is cold,
        And the night bird is whirring
            Uncomfortably in front of your eye.

Translated by Lotte Kramer

Seamus Heaney Centre, School of English, Queen's University

Louis MacNeice:
Centenary Conference & Celebration
12–15 September 2007

'I was born in Belfast between the mountain and the gantries
To the hooting of lost sirens and the clang of trams:
Thence to smoky Carrick in County Antrim…'

(MacNeice, 'Carrickfergus')

Speakers and poets include: Jonathan Allison, Simon Armitage, Terence Brown, Neil Corcoran, Valentine Cunningham, Paul Farley, Michael Longley, Peter McDonald, Medbh McGuckian, Derek Mahon, Sinead Morrissey, Paul Muldoon, Don Paterson, Jon Stallworthy and Clair Wills.

The poet Louis MacNeice was born in Belfast on 12 September 1907. To mark his centenary, the Seamus Heaney Centre is organising a Conference and Celebration at Queen's University. Leading poets, scholars and critics will discuss MacNeice's place in modern poetry. There will be readings by poets from Ireland and Britain who acknowledge him as a hugely influential figure. There will be a tour of places associated with MacNeice in Co. Down and Co. Antrim. All events will be open to the public.

Local & international significance of MacNeice's Centenary

Louis MacNeice's influence, like his poetic landscape, spans these islands and beyond. He was the poet who most immediately absorbed the full legacy of Yeats in the area of Irish poetry. In English poetry, along with Auden, he created the new poetry of the 1930s. MacNeice also exemplifies complexities that centre on Northern Ireland in ways that remain vitally relevant today. To mark the centenary, BBC Northern Ireland is preparing a travelling exhibition on
'Louis MacNeice and the BBC'.

contact: e.longley@qub.ac.uk   website: www.qub.ac.uk/heaneycentre

CENTREFOLD

ℬ

Poetry is the art of saying things once.
—*Don Paterson*

The Lyric Principle
Part 1: The Sense Of Sound

DON PATERSON

These are the first two sections of an essay the concluding instalment of which will appear in the next issue of Poetry Review, 97:3. *They will spend most of their time making and elaborating on some necessary definitions and distinctions; the second instalment will look at technical specifics. It concerns itself with that part of verse-making known as 'lyric', here used in the restricted sense of that aspect of the art that attends to its music, i.e. to the patterning of its sounds. My intention is to demonstrate that language itself has a lyric basis and is itself a poetic system, and that poetry is merely the natural result of language placed under certain kinds formal pressure and emotional urgency. I'm of the opinion that it's impossible to sensibly discuss a single aspect of poetic composition without some reference to all the others, and I haven't tried. I hope the reader will not mistake the tone of relentless asseveration for self-certainty; it's just the quickest way of provoking the sort of constructive disagreement that will allow me to correct my position.*

(i)

Our dominance as a species can be largely blamed on our superior future-predicting capability, a capability derived from and mirrored by the sophistication and length of our memory. Language put us at a terrifically unfair advantage in terms of forward planning, as it allowed us to discuss things in their absence; the biped with the capacity for abstract thought probably wins out all over the universe. To look for the roots of poetry in evolutionary psychology leads us quickly into wilder speculation than even that speculative discipline can accommodate; but based on what we know of its use in more primitive societies, it seems safe enough to assume that poetry was compelled into being, in part at least, through the need for pre-literate cultures to have a mnemonic system of information storage and recovery to supplement that which their minds could comfortably retain. Thus, even in its most primitive form, poetry was concerned with transcending a human limitation: it was a 'magical' art that could conjure from thin air the location of waterholes, hunting grounds and food-stores, the sequenced appearance of plants and flowers, the cycles and lore of weather, season and animal husbandry – as well as the stories, histories and genealogies that served the evolutionarily advantageous purpose of deepening the sense of community and tribe. Poetry, in its *ur*-form of memorizable speech, would then have been deeply connected to the world and our own survival in it; little wonder that it quickly invested *itself* with those magical properties, and also took the form of the spell, the riddle, the curse, the blessing, the prayer. For those deeply atavistic reasons, poetry remains an invocatory form. Prose evokes; the well-chosen word describes the thing as if it were present. But poetry persists in its attempt to *invoke,* to call down its subject from above, as if there were no 'as if' at all. Poetry cannot literally do this, of course; but through the collusion of poet and reader, it can *appear* to, with enough potency to engage our physical senses.

'Magical' practices naturally intermarry, and poetry has long been closely allied with music and song.[1] Music occurs without humans and need only be overheard by them to exist. The wind will whistle up octaves, tonics, dominants, and harmonic overtones; the birds, complex melody. Water dripping from a leaf-tip into a pool will supply a rhythmic series of random intervals around a mean pitch-centre. Elsewhere, music seems waiting to be made: a cut reed just needs us to breath over it to suggest a vertical flute; in some versions of the Greek myth, Hermes discovers the lyre – the very emblem of our guild – when he finds a rotten tortoise-shell, still strung with a few muscle-tendons; recently, I stood in a cave-system in Andalusia where the stalactites had formed a massive floor-length stone drape, each fold of which gave a different gong-like tone when struck. Music has long supplied us with the paradoxical sense of a language that is humanly manipulable and articulate, yet of non-human origin and beyond human words. Music is seemingly precise in its emotional meaning, yet, quite unlike our object-taking word-sense, wholly intransitive and unparaphrasable. When we seek to infuse our speech with a mood or emotion it cannot express, it's to music, to the patterning of sounds, that we instinctively reach.[2] While its signs are somewhat culture-specific (minor keys, for example, will echo different moods in different cultures) we have managed to map the infinitely complex landscape of human emotion to its rather weirdly discarnate medium.

---

1. *Lyric* is of course derived from *lyre*, and *music* from *muse*; *mousike* was a general term which could cover any of the muse-ruled arts or sciences. In Rome, *ars musica* described and conflated both instrumental music and poetry. Mnemosyne, the muse of memory, was the mother of all the other muses; according to Hesiod, both kings and poets arrogated authority to their speech through her possession.
2. This happens long before we're moved to make a song or poem: in our spoken conversation, variations in pitch are responsible for so much of what we convey of our emotional tone, and such subtle sense-making and emphasis as the mere word-sense of our speech will not carry; this is why much sense can still be made of an unintelligible conversation heard through a wall, and why the Daleks have trouble conveying irony.

Song, though, is an uniquely human business. (As beautiful as they are, whale-song and bird-song are largely concerned with territory-marking and sexual selection, and are barely analogous to the signature twitter of our speech, never mind *Winterreise* or *Woodstock*.) Human song is double, and binds an exclusively human system we have developed to a universal one we have merely learned to manipulate. Wedded to music, our speech becomes self-transcending, immediately coupled to a primal and universal realm in which it can symbolically and literally participate.[3] For that reason, perhaps – its ability to unite our choppy and fragmented perception by singing across the gaps – song has long been our aspirational archetype, and in the figure of Orpheus we see the singer defying death itself.[4] Like the musical note, the word is a time-based event; words can be recalled into one another's presence and their meanings yoked together by the careful repetition and arrangement of their sounds.[5] This repetition therefore introduces a real perceptual distortion: it offers a small stay against the *passage* of time, and in its tiny Orphic way, cheats death a little too.

Poetry, then, was an aspirant form, one which sought to transcend human limitations of memory. For a long time it was, in all likelihood, an art barely distinguishable from song.[6] For one thing, the fixing of an already patterned speech to a repeated pattern of set pitches would aid the memory even further. However with the advent of literacy and the concomitant ability to communicate the poem in written form (where pitch height and length cannot be easily indicated), poetry would naturally begin to turn in on itself, and begin to mine its music from its own medium, language.[7] Poetry, though, remains closely linked to the performative physicality of

---

3. For what it's worth, I tend to subscribe to a materialist definition of the aesthetic sublime: those moments we think of as sublimely transcendent are bringing us close not to God but to the earth, with whom we have established a rather distant relationship, and with whom our moments of reunion are so infrequent that they strike us with the force of revelation.

4. Rilke, in particular, sees the Orphic project as one of unifying the temporal and the eternal. I've recently expanded on this at length elsewhere [in the 'Afterword' in *Orpheus* – Ed.].

5. This formula was stolen and adapted from Hugh Kenner. More prosaically: our 7-bit short-term memory encodes information acoustically, our long-term memory semantically. Our sound-tricks simply give the poem a better chance of hooking in on a single hearing.

6. Until very recently, it seems poetic performances remained more-or-less sung: something we hear very clearly in recordings of Tennyson, Yeats and Pound, all of whom centred their recitals on a relatively high fixed pitch, about a fourth or fifth above normal conversation-pitch, and elongated their vowels. Their falling end-of-phrase cadences are all regular and liturgical, not varied and conversational. Pound's immaculate Harry Lauder impersonation remains something of a mystery, however.

7. The song-lyric itself has absolutely no requirement to be particularly musical, in the way that the poem does; from the poet's point of view, the song-lyric can seem an almost negative discipline, in that there are so many effects that it must *avoid* if it isn't to intrude on its setting. With the exception of Burns and a handful of others, poets are rarely selfless enough to suppress their own expertise in this way, and are mostly bad lyricists.

song, and something of its primitive power ebbs away when the connection becomes strained or broken. At the very least, poetry is always highly conscious of the noise it makes.[8]

Poetry also retains its unique and near-magical property: it is the one art form where its memory and its acquisition are one and the same thing. The memory of the symphony, painting, film or novel, however vivid, is no more than that: a memory, or at best a very partial recovery.[9] A story perhaps remains more closely a story, but its structure, not its form of words, remains intact. But if you can remember a poem, you possess it wholly: to remember a poem *is* the poem, and it has become, quite literally, a part of you. Since this is poetry's principal claim on uniquity, any definition of poetry which does not include it remains partial. Because of this strange property, the poem has inevitably tended to valorise or even fetishize those strategies and devices which make it more memorable, in the narrow sense of its ability to be memorised. (Perhaps just because it is so uniquely well-suited to the task, the little time-trap of the poem often takes for its subject-matter that which we feel should be not only remembered, but forcefully memorialised; it does this so frequently that in English, at least, its elegiac tone is pervasive to the point of inaudibility.) This is the case even in an age when its memorisability is no longer a necessity, and something we can delegate to other media besides our own axons, neurons and synapses. However if it loses this, poetry loses one of the most characteristic features of its own identity.

The most powerful mnemonic devices are brief speech, patterned speech, and original speech. Brevity of speech is the poem's most basic formal strategy; originality of speech, its most basic literary virtue; patterned speech, its most basic identifying feature. The mere act of making brief speech often produces both original and patterned speech, the former by expedient necessity, the latter by physical law.[10] All three naturally arise from the compositional process, but we can also employ them as deliberate strategies. Our brevity is specifically achieved with the help of the various tropes of contraction; our originality, with the various tropes of comparison; our patterning, by the parallel schemes of form, metre and

---

8. This is one reason the musical setting of poems is almost invariably a redundant or destructive exercise, resulting in either the contradiction of the original music, or its melodramatic duplication – an exercise akin, in Valery's damning formulation, to 'looking at a painting through a stained glass window'. Composers would do better to find other ways of shaping the air.

9. Exceptions are practitioners: there are visual artists with near-eidetic recall, and composers who can hear seven independent and simultaneous voices.

10. While within the tiny planet of the poem itself there may be all manner of artful excursions, diversions and 'dead lines', the better to disguise its artifice and time its effects – almost all poems are sworn to say what they have to say in as few words as possible, with the possible exception of the hybrid form of verse drama.

sound. (The compositional reality, though, finds all three deeply interwoven.)

The poem tends to originate from an emotionally urgent impulse in the mind of the poet, and simultaneously seeks out and is drawn towards forms which reflect and facilitate that urgency.[11] Language behaves in a curiously material-like way, and placed under the dual pressures of emotional urgency and temporal limit, will reveal its crystalline structure and intimate grain. Poetry only exaggerates and makes manifest features already present in the tongue, and emerges naturally from the language as a simple consequence of emotion, and our urge to communicate it; thus language itself can be fruitfully considered as a coherent poetic system.

The poet's interrogation of language reveals its machinery, which it normally keeps buried and of which we are largely unconscious; this machine is then consciously turned to the making of the poem. Poetry reveals language's underlying metrical regularity, and its tendency to pattern its sounds; it reveals the metaphoric engine by which language revivifies itself, and the synecdochic nature of all human naming (which represents things by declaring an aspect of them that humans find either useful or perceptually salient); it reveals the rhythms that dominate language's natural phrase-lengths and its narrative and argumentative episodes. The sum total of poetry's forms and tropes are no more or less than the natural tendencies and predilections of language made manifest and hardened up to a set of rules.

The poet is engaged in something very closely analogous to trying to remember a poem they have forgotten. While all poetic devices serve to increase the memorability of the poem for the reader (they all play a mnemonic role, in addition to any other purpose they might have served) – for the poet they are the very means, the intuitive tools of retrieval, by which the poem itself is drawn forth from the mind. In others words, all the tropes and schemes that help us achieve our brevity, originality and patterning are really as much *aides-memoires* to the poet as the reader, and their experiences are weirdly mirrored. They are not mere 'effects',[12] but together

---

11. I would generally hold that poems written without feeling teach us very little about poetry, and that it's a bad idea to write a poem if you're not moved to do so; which is why I maintain the unfashionable opinion that writing workshops where poems are actually written amount to little more than a pleasant way of passing the afternoon.

12. Academic accounts of our subject are riddled with many misconceptions, but the identification and discussion of so much intrinsic technique as isolable extrinsic effect is perhaps the most grievous; many of these effects, as described, occur neither in the experience of the poet nor the reader. The poetic effect represents the convergence of twenty different technical and imaginative considerations; between them, these parameters construct the Gestalt within which the poet, often instinctively, makes their beautiful move; thus a *real* description of a compositional decision would have to plot it as a point in multidimensional phase-space. It's obviously necessary to simplify, but we should never do so to the point of lying, and losing track of the fact that poetry is not a series of effects but a dynamic and rich process for both poet and reader.

form the engine of poetic composition itself. For the poet the good poem has the certainty of a thing recalled as true, and they labour towards the final poem as towards a clear and indelible memory. A good poem has the inevitability of truth, and it's hard to conceive of the world having ever been without it – which is why we so often suspect our best lines of having already been written by someone else.

We force ourselves towards a brevity of speech through limiting the time and space in which we have to speak; this constitutes the most basic definition of form, and without its resistance, as Raymond Chandler says, there can be no art. The poem is shaped by a pressured silence; this has rectilinear representation on the page, via the horizontal axis of poem- and stanza-length, and the vertical axis of lineation. Under this pressure, we are immediately compelled towards original speech through simply being forced to choose our words with the utmost economy, since there is no room for redundant elaboration – which would contradict the project of making a unity of our material. (Stanzas, for example, are a way of identifying the episodic rhythm of our poem; their finite length can then operate as an editorial filter for redundancy and irrelevancy.) As Brodsky said so perfectly: "Poetry amounts to arranging words with the greatest specific gravity in the most effective and externally inevitable sequence." The common diagnosis that a poem is 'underpressured' usually means that its elements are not unified by their theme, and their relationships diffuse or underdeveloped.

Soon the poem becomes filled with its symptomatic artifacts: brevity results in calculated elisions, contractions and discontinuities whose meaning we know the reader will be able to infer from our carefully suggested context; originality leaves its rhetorical and syntactic innovations, and its imaginative leaps; patterning leaves its parallel effects of lineation, stanza, rhyme, metre, and consonantal and assonantal echoes. All this leaves us with a piece of text often identifiable as a poem by its brazen lack of self-explanation, its original phrasemaking, and its formal shape. Were we to read this text as a 'normal' piece of prose, we would likely identify these features as, respectively, discontinuous, alien and artificial. The contract of poetry, however, is that we agree to see none of those things, but instead a wholly natural language-game in which poet and reader collude.

However this often leaves the reader with far more work to do than in a piece of prose (the patterning often seems to me a sort of sensual sweetener for that work), and therefore – since each individual will inevitably bring different responses as they meet the poem half-way, in their own way – poetry by its very nature has an inbuilt 'difficulty', or, if you flip it round, a non-fixity of interpretation. Crucially, this interpretative freedom also permits *ownership* of the poem at a much deeper level through the personalization of its meaning. The poem also works through a subtle appeal to the ego: we ally the desirable object of the well-made poem to the promise of personal relevance, our poem's concern with the reader themselves. This aids its memorability as much as any of our mnemonic trickery.

However the poem must furthermore *be identifiable as such* for the game to begin; the poem is as much a mode of reading as writing. The reader must know they are reading a poem to read-it-as-a-poem, and apply all their remarkable human powers of signification and connection.[13] (All the more so, since in the pursuit of an aesthetic naturalism, some of the most artful poems have the habit of disguising themselves as far simpler statements than they really are.) Our formal patterning most often supplies a powerful typographical advertisement. What it advertises most conspicuously is that the poem has not taken up the whole page, and considers itself somewhat important. The white space around the poem then becomes a potent symbol of the poem's significant intent. This white space is both literally and symbolically equivalent to silence.

Silence is the poet's ground. It's silence that delineates the formal borders of the poem, and the formal arrangement of silences that puts the language under the pressure of its form. Silence – both invoked and symbolized by the white page, and specifically directed by the gaps left by lineation, stanza and poem – underwrites the status of the poem as *significant mark*. This mark explicitly invites the reader to attend to the poem in such a way as permits it its full resonant potential, both acoustically and semantically, as a voice within an auditorium. In doing so it also declares our master trope, that of synecdoche – the business of representing a whole by a smaller part. Almost all poetry operates under such an understanding, i.e. that it is a small thing which stands for a larger, and that it has more *significance* than a piece of prose with the same word-count would have, simply because the reader has been specifically directed to *find* more

---

13. Humans – no doubt in an act of vital compensation for their habit of hypercategorization, and the fragmented perception it brings – will connect any two unrelated things you care to throw at them. This is neatly demonstrated in the old workshop game where a noun randomly receives the definition of a completely different one. The reader almost invariably makes it fit by ransacking the noun's internal properties, aspects and relations until they have found several points of coincidence or imaginative possibility, and it transpires that a keyhole *is*, in a sense, a square box in which one watches moving pictures, or that a mouse *is* a form of public transport that runs on rails. What is astonishing is a) the degree to which this process is instinctive and instantaneous and b) the extent to which everything seems to be secretly related. When the poem is too discontinuous and insufficient context has been provided to link its elements, the reader compensates by sending their connecting faculty into overdrive, and starts finding connections and significances for which they were given absolutely no cue. Incidentally, the various types of confident misreading that can then result – for which the poet is often to blame – are, somewhat terrifyingly, aptly and neatly described in the terminology of clinical paranoia. But that's for another time.

significance than its mere prose sense gives. (Heaven help the poet if the reader turns that expectation into time invested, then discovers that the poem is found wanting.) Silence is the acoustic space in which the poem makes its large echoes. If you want to test this, write a single word on a blank sheet of paper and stare at it: note the superior attendance to the word the silence insists upon, and how it soon starts to draw out the word's ramifying sense-potential, its etymological story, its strange acoustic signature, its calligraphic mark; you are reading the word as poetry.

Since it is silence that lends our poems their significant look, and so quietly prompts the reader to being their act of poetic signifying, poets go to great lengths to summon and honour it with bold and discrete sounds. Spoil it with extraneous chatter, inadvertent repetition, superfluous qualifiers, nervous and unnecessary glosses, or worst, with ugly accidental noise – and the ground of the silence is stained, the sense of the word as a distinct acoustic event is wrecked, and all subtle lyric patterning inaudible. Worst of all our synecdoche – precisely, the *spell* of the poem – is fatally weakened as the poem's status is undermined. We maintain the spell most effectively by balancing that unity of silence by a reciprocal unity of utterance; the latter has the strange effect of raising the former.

A poetic form is essentially a codified pattern of silence. We have a little silence at the end of the line, a bigger one at the end of a stanza, and a huge one at the end of the poem. The semantic weight of the poem tends to naturally distribute itself according to that pattern of silence, paying especial care to the sounds and meanings of the words and phrases that resonate into the little empty acoustic of the line-ending, or the connecting hallway of stanza-break, or the big church of the poem's end. These silences are where all the interesting things often tend to bunch up, to take advantage of the acoustic salience they enjoy in this position – and with which the natural closures of phrase-length and episode tend to coincide.[14]

The white page is also sign to the reader that our poems were *won* from silence, drawn out from it – when we went there, and sat in the as-yet-consonant-free breath of our inspiration, and began to try and articulate the inarticulable, those beyond-words relations and feelings, and then were granted a few strange words that seemed to adhere to them. Hence the strangeness of our speech; unable either to invent a new language or resort to a pure music or glossolalia, our words are forced into original combinations to increase their expressive possibilities – but they would still

---

14. An ignorance of this tendency, and the subsequent inability to challenge it, can lead to tediously repetitive tics in some authors; they fail to naturalize the form. Most poets will instinctively use occasional enjambment, and occasionally *not* put the most interesting word as teleuton, for the sake of natural variation.

perhaps appear too alien, were they not unified through our lyric strategies. We turn naturally towards music as an intercessory channel between the familiar and the strange, and use it to bind our sense with a pervasive strength that syntax alone cannot accomplish.

What the silence *itself* invokes is, and should probably remain, a matter of personal conviction. For what it's worth – for this author, it seems to stand for a realm of perception where all things are connected as they were in our very early childhood, before the fall into time and category, a fall brutally reinforced by the acquisition of language. Without making the distinction between self and other, mother and breast, sky and earth, without the clear differentiation of things, there can there can be no proper experience of their temporal or causal sequence, and hence we had a different perception of time passing. This place of atemporal and infinite connection still exists, running like a operating system upon which the more recently acquired software of perceptual category and language sits. Poetry is one means by which we can still access it, and I suspect our meditations, if not quite 'the place that poems come from', then at least allow us to enter a space where new and original connections are forged beyond language, and find their linguistic incarnation at its very limits. Lurking behind this connecting silence is a brooding suspicion over the extent to which the perceptual user-preferences of the human animal limit and distort its experience of reality, and the consequently unreliable nature of much of its thought. Poetry is the means by which we correct the main tool of that thought, language, for its anthropic distortions: it is language's self-corrective function, and everywhere challenges our Adamite inheritance – the catastrophic, fragmenting design of our conceptualising machinery – through the insistence on a counterbalancing project, that of lyric unity.[15] (What we call 'poetry' is only really a salience; language has poetry built into it like the body has the endocrine system.) If we remember that all light we supposedly shed on the universe is of a hopelessly human hue, we can compensate for its little spectrum, and accept the partiality of what it reveals; we do this by singing of the larger unity of which it is merely a synecdochic expression.

Anyway, to summarise: between the invisible master trope of synecdoche, our sworn law of brevity, and our project of honouring the silence that makes our poems poems, we subject our poetic speech to a pressure that requires it to unite its constituent elements at a far deeper and more integrated level than one would normally encounter in the mainly linear narrative and argumentative structures of prose. In short: to save

---

15. It's amusing to think that if physics succeeds in its attempts to find some vibrational basis for the universe in the form of string or membrane – i.e. proves that difference itself is a mere manifestation of frequency-rates – it will be consubstantial with the lyric project, that is to say it will show it to be *non-symbolic*.

space, we must introduce an additional dimensionality of meaning: we can't build out, so we must build up. (Or, if I can be forgiven one musical analogy – we now have to insist that our lines have harmonic and contrapuntal depth, as well as melodic interest.)

(ii)

The first step towards this complexity of implication and interrelation is the minimization of the number of thematic elements, whose relationships cannot deepen in their intricacy and sophistication while the elements themselves multiply.[16] Having done this, the most economic and instinctively natural way to then accomplish this sophistication and complexity is through a shift in emphasis from denotative to connotative meaning. (This is something that all poems demonstrate that ally themselves with the lyric tradition, which is to say all poems that do not deliberately reject it.) Since poems have to say an awful lot in a short space, connotation is at a premium, as it multiplies relations, not terms; it functions, effectively, as an incredibly subtle and pervasive unifying force, a sort of secret trope of contraction. As I'll show, we find this reflected in and effected by the poem's obsessive patterning of sound. By this I certainly don't just mean rhyme, or loud effects like alliteration, but the use of far quieter patterns, often achieved instinctively by the poet and registered subliminally by the reader. These I'll detail later.

The denotative meaning of a word is singular; the connotative meaning of a word is potentially infinite, and contains all possible terms. However those terms are strongly centred upon its core denotation, its designated referent (i.e. the fruit 'apple' for the word 'apple'), and those *properties* without which this referent is impossible.[17] But beyond that, there exists a penumbra of strongly associated aspects, less strongly consensually fixed than its denotation. We tend to also think of the apple as having the qualities of being round, tree-grown, red or green or brown in colour, and sweet and

---

16. This is a complex subject and will be explored elsewhere, but briefly: having learnt the trick of murdering one's darlings (with Occam's Razor, I guess) early in the poem's draft, a more subtle project then emerges. In pursuit of its unity, it's usually the goal of the poetic line to avoid understatement and overstatement, that is – to say a thing cleanly, once, and then run away. Poetry is the art of saying things once. The sin, for a decent poet, is not saying a thing twice, or failing to say it at all, which are beginner's errors: the problem is saying things 0.8 or 1.3 times. What counts as a helpful gloss in prose is often an intolerable pleonasm in poetry; we don't have the time.
17. These are things we never think about: the hypernymic sets to which we agree 'apple' must probably belong - 'a fruit'; 'a thing grown', etc., but also those properties without which the thing becomes unthinkable as itself. It's impossible, for example, to write 'ping-pong ball' and mean something with a wholly solid interior, or 'window' and mean a thing which admits no light; if we wanted to communicate those things, we would have to do so by unambiguous qualification.

sharp to the taste (though unlike the inconceivable non-fruit apple, we can conceive, at a pinch, of a square or even a blue one). These secondary aspects radiate out, weakening in strength as they pass from rigid designation, to consensual agreement, to the random valencies of personal association and memory. Unlike its single and often unique denotation, the set of any word's close connotations will, of course, contain many terms which will overlap with those possessed with many others: apples share their qualities of roundness and sweetness and redness with a thousand other things.

A word's strong connotations, its immediate circle of strong aspects, relations and associations, are what gives it its 'feel', but not its dictionary definition.[18] The 'feel' of words concerns the poet every bit as much as their dictionary meaning. Overlaps in 'feel' between words – their shared quality of roundness, shortness, sharpness, bluntness, brevity, lightness, brightness – are very often betrayed by a common sound, regardless of the sense-realm to which the word belongs. This statement continues to be heretical in certain quarters, but it lies behind the poet's operative conceit and fundamental article of faith, which is that *sound and sense are aspects of the same thing*. In the poem's composition, we often allow sound to guide us to sense, and vice-versa: the ear can be trusted to think, and the mind to hear. We make our decisions within a phonosemantic system, where the 'rightness' of a word or line is verified as much by its sound as its meaning, and within which *we are never forced to choose one over the other*; logically, such a contradiction cannot arise, as the two are merely manifest aspects of a same thing.

Whenever we encounter two things in nature which share a form – a brain and a cauliflower, the sea and the wind in a cornfield, an ear and a bean, a bean and a foetus, a tree or a nerve, a nerve and a tributary system – we unthinkingly assume some kind of strongly analogous relation between the dynamic forces that produced them.[19] By and large such instinctive assumptions are reasonable and well-founded. But for some reason language is regarded as a special case, and we have been instructed to regard many of its sound-symmetries as accidental – despite the fact that language, like everything else in this place – from the paperclip and the bomb, to the rose and Cepheid variable – naturally arose. However when we initially encounter those symmetries, we have no inhibitions in hearing declared not

---

18. Dictionaries are of course concerned with denotation only, and have to coyly circle around their referents by naming the fewest number of strong aspects and connotations required to narrow the possibilities to one; it's no use saying an apple is an apple. This offers a rather large clue to the nature of the onomastic process itself.

19. Once, on top of Pen y Fan, I found ice clinging to some grass stalks that had been blown to immaculate bird-feathers, the wind and water between them having whistled up a form in a few hours that had taken several million years to evolve.

just an acoustic relation, but a dynamic relation of evolved sense. You know this when you're three years old, and you go *mum / tum / thumb / bum!* for the first time, and are delighted not just because they all sound similar, but all have the same rounded and warm feel about them.

The semantic unit in denotative speech is the morpheme; the semantic unit in poetic, connotative speech is the phoneme. That 'words seem to sound like the thing they mean' is something long understood instinctively, and has been chewed over since the Cratylus dialogue. Yet it's difficult to prove: because we're dealing with 'feel', we can only point to tendencies, not rules. As a result, even this late in the day, we still have to listen to folk harping on about the arbitrariness of the sign, which poets know to be sheer madness.[20] The idea holds up well for merely denotative speech – and indeed were language a matter of simple designation, if we all agreed to call a cup a banana, a banana it would be. But it would *feel* wrong, and for reasons other than our mere cultural acclimation to cuppiness of 'cup'. (Scientific speech is of necessity almost wholly denotative, and free of all the productive ambiguities poets love; it's also, alas, the sort of speech most linguisticians use, and still instinctively privilege.)

The term 'iconicity' refers to the physical sound of a word enacting its referent. Until fairly recently, it was primarily used to describe onomatopoeia, where 'thump' sounds like a thump, 'clatter' like a clatter, and 'bark' like a bark. Understandably, given this narrow interpretation, it has been easy to dismiss as the relatively trivial effect of 'sound symbolism'. Mercifully, this is changing, and the science is slowly catching up with our poetic intuitions, especially in the field of phonosemantics. Much of this is taken up with the study of 'phonesthemes', which are of particular interest to us: a phonestheme is a point of sound-sense coincidence. A standard example is the sound *gl-*, which occurs in a disproportionately high number of words related to 'light' and 'sight' to be mere chance: *glisten, glare, glow, glower, glint, gleam, glaze, gloss, glance, glitter*. Many words which contain the sound *unk – bunk, sunk, puncture, dunk, lunk, trunk, funk* – even though etymologically unrelated, all have a low, sunken, heavy, concave 'feel' to

---

20. Saussure wasn't, actually, quite so sure as he is often made out to be, but the 'arbitrariness' line is maintained through Chomsky, and even to such otherwise enlightened commentators as Steven Pinker – this despite brilliant corrective interventions, by Roman Jakobson in particular. Folk know themselves in strange ways, and Saussure had a good idea, I think, of the monstrous dogma he had proposed. Towards the end of his life – in what I like to think of as a paranoid act of guilty compensation – he was tormented by an unusual demon; his kabbalistic and obsessive hobby was to search texts for anagrams, which, once uncovered, would reveal the author's true unconscious intentions. Of course this means looking for specific *sounds*, the dispersal of which would reveal deeper *meaning* than any analysis of morphemes alone could possibly permit; forty years later, and he'd have been playing Beatles records backwards. He'd have been better off, one is forced to reflect, writing a poem instead.

them. Some think the number of such phonesthemes is finite; it seems clear to me – and I suspect to most poets – that the phonestheme is merely the most obvious symptom of a fundamental and wholly pervasive rule of language.

Counterexamples seem easy to give, but prove nothing. This is because language works on a *diffuse* synaesthetic principle of connotation, a broad iconicity. Sounds invoke things not only in their sound, if they are fortunate enough to make one – but in *any aspect*: their visual appearance, smell, shape and function. We hear the roundness of *moon*, the warmth of *mum*,[21] the ruminativeness of *memory*, the hiss of *sea*, the thinness of *needle*, the lumpiness of *hump*, the speed of *quick*. Language works in part by synaesthetic analogue: through the brain's automatic habit of synaesthetic mapping, 'brightness' is a property not only of light, but of sound, shape, taste, emotional mood, and so on, and this is reflected in our speech. Poetry, as usual, refines a linguistic tendency to a strategy.[22]

There is no doubt that one reason for phonesthemes arising is simply the clustering of sounds, through familiar association, to part-arbitrary tongue-specific conventions of usage; but elsewhere (crucially, this is borne out by interlingual studies – the short *i* phonestheme is pretty much universally associated with lightness, brevity, smallness) they seem to suggest that the shapes of sounds in the mouth formed naturally as physical analogues to the shapes of real things and processes in the world. These two forces are probably impossible to separate out. It's hard, in other words, to establish whether many English words that begin with the sound *sn-* carry the connotations 'nose' because there is something in this human sound that mimics a reality, or because they have helplessly converged on an arbitrary English convention; the truth is probably somewhere in between.

(Our habit of synaesthetic representation may be close to a receiving a proper explanation. V.S. Ramachandran has argued that it has its origins in crosstalk between the various sense-centres in the modular architecture of the brain, and in exaptation, i.e. taking expedient advantage of neural

---

21. A classic example of words arising through environmental expedience: the word for 'mother' in most languages contains the m- sound, the only noise the child can make at the breast. There is a well-known and bizarre exception: in Georgian, mother is 'deda'. This is only partly explained by the obvious choice being already taken by their word for father, 'mama'.

22. One still occasionally meets the objection that a thing or event which makes no sound cannot possibly have a sound to represent it; the trouble is that the 'definition' of a phonestheme indicates not rigid designation but a mere statistical tendency, its sound denoting an area of overlapping connotatory sense between several different words. The word 'meaning' can't be honestly used of a phonestheme either, since 'meaning' implies a clear denotation; it has no meaning, only a consensual 'feel', upon which the words that host it converge.

pathways evolution had previously opened up for other purposes. Language itself may have come about through just such a synaesthetic transfer: a hand-signal shaped in imitation of a real form could be instinctively doubled by an analogous mouth-shape, especially when a cry was being made anyway to reinforce the gesture.)

As we now know, new coinages will naturally and unconsciously gravitate towards the active and attractive nodes of certain phonesthemes as a way of deepening their sense. This means that iconicity is 'strong' as well as broad.[23]

For example the word 'blog' is felicitous – if ugly – not just because it's a contraction of 'weblog'; it carries the echoes of *bl-* and *-og* phonesthemes. *Bl-* has a feel of 'speechiness', around which we find clustered *blather, blab, blow, blame, blah, blurt, blurb, blub, bluster, bless, blether, blast, bleat*; also less strongly of 'bluntness', as in *blunt, bluff, blow*. *-og* has a low, crude feel of 'blockage' found in too many *-og* and *-g* words to list. (This latter echo is probably semi-knowingly facetious, as in the revolting contraction 'spag bol'. You can see how quickly all this can descend into idle – if enjoyable –

---

23. I have the suspicion that as language developed, the emergent property of broad and systematic iconicity reified to the extent that it began to exert, through a process of downward causality, a supervenient influence on language itself. The system now positively charged with iconic intent, the phonestheme – instead of being merely a passively-arising index of shared aspect – would then start to exert an active, gravitational pull: words which share the phoneme now exhibit a real, if thin, semantic connection *regardless* of their initial unrelatedness: that such a sense is apparitional is an impossible accusation in a closed system. As the iconic effect became wholly pervasive, any word, however apparently 'arbitrary' in its sound-sense relation, would then exert some tiny influence on the whole system: in other words 'apple' starts to *sound* like an apple, and contributes its own micro-phonestheme, however weakly, to all other occurrences of the same phonemes in the language, which then all carry the ghost of 'appleness', with the valency now primed to increase as the two words increase in spoken proximity. (It's interesting to speculate whether 'synaesthically unseeded' artificial systems, like John Wilkins' philosophical language, could ever enjoy even a weak emergent iconicity.) Read this way, the phonestheme becomes merely a salience in a disease-of-degree game, and words themselves sit at the convergence of many more influences than merely a couple of governing phonesthemes. Who can say if 'glue' has not taken on a little sheen from its 'unrelated' *gl*-bearing 'bright' words, or 'sneak' a little nasality from *sn*-bearing 'nosy' words - or indeed apple from the *p–* phonesthemes related to 'pulling' 'stealing' 'picking' and 'quiet noise'? Were we able to submit words to the same spectral analysis we can the sounds of a musical instrument, we would see an extremely complex additive pattern of semantic overtone, from strong partials to almost impossibly weak upper harmonics. The picture is further complicated because language is a dynamic system, and each word changes according to its contextual employment, i.e. its site-specific sense, and its 'semantic infection' from its near neighbours. (This is *particularly* true in the poem, where context is rigged, and just such 'infection' is intended by its phonic patterning. Put 'pale' and 'apple' in the same line, and they conjure a ghost-phonestheme between them, and their senses are a little interfused; put them together, and their iconizing valencies virtually allow them to form a single new word. I realize I've buried this secret formula here so that no one will read it.) Thus this spectrograph would – while perhaps fairly constant in its fundamental of denoted sense – register constant change in its upper partials. We have no need to muddy the waters further by introducing other parameters like regional variation and personal association. Essentially, no sense steps into the same word twice.

speculation, and how important statistical studies are in lending the subject any legitimacy.) Phonosemantic felicity is the precise analogue here of evolutionary fitness, and simply gives a new word a better chance of survival.[24]

The standard objection is that the world cannot imprint itself on speech, because it's not universally consistent: a dog and a tree is pretty much a dog and a tree wherever you go, but the sounds we make to indicate for 'dog' or 'tree' are completely different in different languages, and therefore must be arbitrary. But this gets it wrong in two ways: firstly – to get the feel of a phonestheme, we look at common *tendencies* in the set of words in which the sound occurs, not in any single word (there is no reason it should actually *exist* in any single word as part of its primary denotation, and these are hardest to spot). Secondly – human designation is aspectual and synecdochic. Take the word *tree* in different sign languages: in American, you shape the wind in the branches; in Chinese, you shape the trunk; in both cases the form itself has clearly imprinted itself on the language, but the point is that it has done so *aspectually*. The aspect is soon forgotten and overtaken by its referent; both signs simply mean 'tree'. This is bound to happen to speech in the same way. We may well make-a-noise-like-the-thing by instinctively forming a shape in the mouth, tongue, teeth, palate and lips to make a synaesthetic echo of something in the real world; but because the things themselves are complex in their aspectual properties, the chances are that we'll often get a very different sounding sign. Aspect is immediately overtaken through cultural exigency by the referent, and what may have began life as a word with a phonestheme bearing the connotation 'shiny' or 'round' or 'white' or 'light' or 'seeing', is suddenly, and exclusively, the word for 'moon'. (This illustrates the primacy, incidentally, of metonymic process.) None of this means the sign is less beautifully fit, and arguments over which tongue has the loveliest word for 'love' or 'moon' are insane: their referent might be the same, but the secret etymology of their phonosemantic history and present connotations to which they have led will

---

24. As the neologism to the language, so the word to the line: to paraphrase Valéry, the prosaic truth is that poets will often be finished with a poem but for one perfectly-fitted word: an anapest, whose contents probably contain a long O, a sibilant, a liquid and a p or a b, and which has something to do with fish.

25. Take the fact that words in different languages can have the same referent, but very different connotations, and the fact that poetry operates on a phonosemantic principle expressly *designed* to take advantage of those connotations within its own language, and you have perhaps the most concise explanation for the sheer 'impossibility' of poetic translation. How can one hope to render the beauty, for example, of cipőfüző, the word voted the most beautiful in the Hungarian language? ('Shoelaces', in case you were wondering.) Incidentally, here I have deliberately and mendaciously avoided a hugely complicating factor: most words sit at the top of a huge pile of dead metaphors (dead referents, strictly speaking), thousands of years old. Our lexeme may have fallen very far from the tree indeed.

differ wildly. [25] Language would *have* to begin with naming a connotation, as no denotation yet exists; denotations have to be forged, whereas connotations naturally arise through the porousness of our receptive senses.

The iconizing engine, the tendency to declare a kinship of sense between words through shared features of their sounds, is deeply embedded in the structure of language. But iconicity is an active as well as a passive principle: words are so *indivisibly* part-sound and part-sense that the patterning of sound alone can generate sense *as if it constituted a syntactic relation*. In our speech we naturally pattern sound to unite sense all the time, forging ghost-phonesthemes from the air: the guy who wrote the chalkboard outside the station pub in Dundee did not hesitate to put FINE WINES GREAT BEERS. GREAT WINES FINE BEERS never entered his head; it's not only less euphonious, its meaning is simply less integrated. The words we choose to convey the most urgent and convincing senses automatically tend to exhibit a higher level of musical organization. As Bill Clinton said so movingly: "Painful as the condemnation of the Congress would be, it would pale in comparison to the consequences of the pain I have caused my family. There is no greater agony." I won't pull the cheap stunt of lineating this to reinforce the point, but his words are fairly astonishing in the coherence of their patterning, and riff virtuosically around the stops *k/g* and *p/b*, and a couple of whimpering nasals. This was not done, you may be certain, to impress us with his lyric prowess.

Regardless of the presence of a 'real' phonestheme or not, words which share sounds, when brought into close proximity, will appear to be united in their sense. Sentences which exhibit a strong sound-pattern will even seem to have a semantic coherence even if they are sheer nonsense. This is why poetry integrates its music. It does more than sound pretty: next to the synecdochic conceit that rules the poem, lyric is our most powerful tool of semantic contraction and integration, of sense-unity and emphasis. (If you want to trick a reader into thinking your terrible poem makes a little sense: rhyme it.) [26]

Denotative sense is capable of decent paraphrase. Connotative sense is not. It isn't articulable in the same way, because it has no synonyms, just unique patterns of relations. The degree of semantic bleed *between* words in denotative speech is far lower, as its aim is one of differentiation, not connection; poetry is concerned with both. In poetry, the semantic blurring is encouraged partly by its tactical elisions, which force the collusion of the reader in its sense-making project – but largely conducted by the patterned phoneme, leaving a statement which, while easily paraphrasable in that

---

26 An unrhymed *Lear*, for example, would be an unthinkable horror.

denotative sense-making part,[27] also has a highly complex sense which is wholly tied to its site-specific physical expression. Poetic meaning pours across the word-boundaries carried by the patterning of its sounds, and often unites its lines as if they were a single word. Because of this, form and content have something of the inseparability we find in a piece of music.

In conclusion: the patterning of sound is a virtual necessity in *any* short speech which seeks to integrate its elements at the deepest level and maximize its resonant potential. Since the writing of a poem often consists in attempting to unify elements we had previously thought of as contradictory, contrasting, unrelated or mutually exclusive, it's of central importance. You might say that poets are trying to make one big, musically coherent unit, in order to conjure up a thing, a state or relation that is new to language, but whose integrity makes it verifiably true in the heart and mind of the reader – with more semantic coherence than the refusal of this lyric strategy could possibly allow. Perhaps we are trying to make one big word out of everything. This means we can trust our ears to do much of the thinking, since we know that if we can tie the word into the lyric weave, its borders have been opened, and its meaning will then seep into the entire poem and serve to unify its total sense.

Everything is driven towards a state of entropy, and yet everywhere matter reflects a weird state of order still inscribed in it by the primal singularity, our unbroken cosmic egg, and falls into wave, sphere, orbit, season and pulse. So do we, and so in turn does our complex system of language, which is as deeply wrought with those symmetric whorls and rhythms and patterns as we are. Poetry discloses all this, and in doing so sings the underlying unity, the same song under everything, the concentric circles that miraculously appear in your coffee mug when you tap the desk. Nonetheless, it's sad to find yourself born into a universe founded on the principle of *nostalgia*. But it's a good place for elegists, perhaps.

---

27. To say a poem can have no paraphrase is to credit it *only* with connotation, which is plain bananas. This, however, is precisely the position I've often encountered students adopt when asked what their poem *means*. (Mostly I get variations on Eliot's dodgy comeback, along the lines of "It means what it means, Mr Paterson; had I meant something different I would have said so just as obscurely," etc. which at least indicates the source of the problem: sloppy interpretations of a received modernist aesthetic.) While no poet should know precisely what they mean before they begin – if writing a poem isn't a way of working out what you mean, then I don't know what it is – they know, mostly, in the end. If they genuinely know nothing, it is an admission that the poem is meaningless. No one is pretending for a moment that a paraphrase or an abstract *is* the poem, any more than a synopsis is a novel: it merely articulates or at least adumbrates the ideas that the poem, singularly and inimitably, has bodied forth. The idea alone has no intrinsic poetic worth, and indeed if you get a good idea for a poem, run a mile. In my own experience – while students often genuinely don't know what their poems mean – all poets can at least tell you what theirs are about. They just don't want to. A poem with no denotative paraphrasable sense is called a sound poem, and it is the only legitimate exception.

Some Notes On Poetry And Religion

CHRISTIAN WIMAN

A rt is like Christianity in this way: at its greatest, it can give you access to the deepest suffering you imagine – not necessarily dramatic suffering, not necessarily physical suffering, but the suffering that is in your nature, the suffering of which you must be conscious to fulfill your nature – and at the same time provide a peace that is equal to that suffering. The peace is not in place of the sorrow; the sorrow does not go away. But there is a moment of counterbalance between them that is both absolute tension and absolute stillness. The tension is time. The stillness is eternity. With art, this peace is passing and always inadequate. But there are times when the very splendid insuffiency of art – its "sumptuous destitution", in Dickinson's phrase – can point a person toward a *peace that passeth understanding*: George Herbert, Marilynne Robinson, T. S. Eliot...

*

Language can create faith but can't sustain it. This is true of all human instruments; which can only gesture toward divinity, never apprehend it. This is why reading the Bible is so often a frustrating, even spiritually estranging, experience. Though you can feel sometimes (particularly in the Gospels) the spark that started a fire of faith in the world – or in your heart – the bulk of the book is cold ash. Thus we are by our own best creations confounded: that Creation, in which our part is integral but infinitesimal, and which we enact by imagination but cannot hold in imagination's products, may live in us. God is not the things whereby we imagine Him.

*

You cannot really know a religion from the outside. That is to say, you can know everything about a religion – its history, iconography, scripture, etc. – but all of that will remain inert, mere information, so long as it is, to you, myth. To have faith in any religion is to accept at some primary level that its particular language of words and symbols says something true about reality. This doesn't mean that the words and symbols *are* reality (that's fundamentalism), nor that you will ever master those words and symbols well enough to regard reality as some fixed thing. What it does mean, though, is that "you can no more be religious in general than you can speak language in general" (George Lindbeck), and that the only way to deepen your knowledge and experience of ultimate divinity is to deepen your knowledge and experience of the all-too-temporal symbols and language of a *particular* religion. Lindbeck would go so far as to say your religion of origin has such a bone-deep hold on you that, as with a native language, it's your only hope for true religious fluency. I wouldn't go that far, but I would say that one has to submit to symbols and language which may be inadequate in order to have those inadequacies transcended. This is true of poetry, too: I do not think you can spend your whole life questioning whether language can represent reality. At some point, you have to believe that the inadequacies of the words you use will be transcended by the faith with which you use them. You have to believe that poetry has some reach into reality itself – or you have to go silent.

*

I think it is a grave mistake for a writer to rely on the language of a religion in which he himself does not believe. You can sense the staleness and futility of an art that seeks energy in gestures and language that are, in the artist's life, inert. It feels like a failure of imagination, a shortcut to a transcendence that he either doesn't really buy, or has not earned in his work. Of course, exactly what constitutes 'belief' for a person is a difficult question. One man's anguished atheism may get him closer to God than another man's mild piety. There is more genuine religious feeling in Phillip Larkin's godless despair and terror than there is anywhere in late Wordsworth.

*

I don't mean to suggest that Larkin was a Christian without knowing it. Milosz does something along these lines with Camus ("if he rejected God it was out of love for God because he was not able to justify Him"), and it seems awfully close to spiritual condescension. Similarly, I once heard someone respond to Larkin's 'Aubade' by saying that, while undeniably beautiful and moving, the poem illustrated perfectly the condition of any person who did not accept Christ. This just won't do. It's not sufficient for Christianity to stand outside of the highest achievements of secular art and offer a kind of pitying, distancing admiration. If Christianity is to have any contemporary meaning at all, it must contain, be adequate to, and inextricable from, modern consciousness; rather than simply retreating into antiquated beliefs and rituals. And modern consciousness is marked by nothing so much as consciousness of death. Can one believe in Christ and death in equal measure? Is this degree of negative capability possible? Paul Tillich pushes toward it in theology, as do, in very different ways, Jurgen Moltman and Dietrich Bonhoeffer, but I can't think of any English-language poets after Eliot who have achieved this (or even tried).

*

Poetry is not written out of despair, which in its pure form is absolutely mute. The poetry that *seems* to come out of despair – Larkin's 'Aubade', for instance, or late Plath – is actually a means of staving it off. A negative charge, simply by virtue of realizing itself, of coming into existence, becomes a positive charge. Whole lives happen this way, sustained by art in which, at some deep level, life is denied. There can be real courage in such lives and art, though it is very easy to move from engaging despair to treasuring it, to slip from necessity into addiction. This is when poetry's powers begin to fail.

*

Art needs some ultimate concern, to use Tillich's phrase. As belief in God waned among late-nineteenth- and early twentieth-century artists, death became their ultimate concern. Dickinson, Stevens, Beckett, Camus – these are the great devotional poets of death. Postmodernism sought to eliminate death in the frenzy of the instant, to deflect it with irony and hard-edged surfaces in which, because nothing was valued more than anything else, nothing was subject to ultimate confirmation or denial. This was a retreat from the cold eye cast on death by the modernists, and the art of postmodernism is, as a direct consequence, vastly inferior. I suspect that the only possible development now is to begin finding a way to once more imagine ourselves into and out of death, though I also feel quite certain that the old religious palliatives, at least those particularly related to the specifically Christian idea of Heaven, are inadequate.

*

"Death is the mother of beauty" is a phrase that could only have been written by a man for whom death was an abstraction, a vaguely pleasant abstraction at that. That's not really a critique of 'Sunday Morning', one of the greatest poems of the twentieth century. Death is an abstraction for all of us; until it isn't. But for the person whose death is imminent and inescapable, nothing is more offensive, useless, or wrong-headed than phrases like "Death is the mother of beauty".

Remove futurity from experience and you leach meaning from it just as surely as if you cut out a man's past. "Memory is the basis of individual personality," Miguel de Unamuno writes, "just as tradition is the basis of the collective personality of a people. We live in memory, and our spiritual life is at bottom simply the effort of our memory to persist, to transform itself into hope, the effort of our past to transform itself into our future." In other words, we need both the past and the future to make our actions and emotions and sensations mean anything in the present.

Strictly speaking, though, the past and the future do not exist. They are both, to a greater or lesser degree, creations of the imagination. Anyone who tells you that you can live only in time, then, is not quite speaking the truth; since if we do not live *out* of time imaginatively, we cannot live *in* it actually. And if we can live out of time in our daily lives – indeed, if apprehending and inhabiting our daily lives *demands* that we in some imaginative sense live out of time – then is it a stretch to imagine the fruition of existence as being altogether outside of time?

Death is the mother of beauty? No, better to say that beauty is the mother of death, for it is the splendour of existence that so fires the imagination forward and backward into our own unbeing. It is the beauty of the world that makes us more conscious of death, not the consciousness of death that makes the world more beautiful.

*

I always find it a little strange to meet a poet for whom religion holds no instinctive resonance whatsoever. Most poets are sympathetic to the miraculous in all its forms, though they are also usually quite promiscuous with their sympathies. Still, there are exceptions. Thom Gunn used to say that there wasn't a religious bone in his body, and I can't recall a single instance from his work that uses religious language as a shortcut to the ineffable. (For an absolutely scrupulous use of religious language and imagery by an unbeliever, look at 'In Santa Maria del Popolo'.) On the other hand, Gunn's work is virtually devoid of mystery (look at 'In Santa Maria del Popolo'). It does not contain (or aim for) moments of lyric transcendence; it offers no ontological surprises. This is not necessarily a specifically religious distinction. Larkin, though his work is absolutely rooted in reality, and though it seems quite clear he didn't believe there was anything beyond it, could never completely repress that part of himself that yearned for transcendence, and his work is full of moments in which clarity of vision and spiritual occlusion combine to mysterious lyric effect. In Gunn's work, by contrast, you sense that there was no hunger which the world could not satisfy.

*

Among the saddest things I know are the words Keats is reputed to have uttered just before he died: "I feel the terrible want of some faith, something to believe in now. There must be such a book." Part of the pathos here is simply the fear and hunger; it is horrible to watch someone die in a rage of unbelief, and there is every reason to think that, had he lived a normal life, Keats would have come to a different accommodation with death, either with or without religious faith. Another part of the pathos though is in the fact that even here, even on his deathbed, Keats can only imagine deliverance as a book, as literature. Keats was a large-souled, warm-hearted, altogether companionable person, but the tragedy of his death was that he did not have a chance to outgrow his youthful devotion to 'poetry' – to the idea of it, I mean. You cannot devote your life to an abstraction. Indeed, life shatters all abstractions in one way or another, including *words* like 'faith' or 'belief'.

*

It is common for people to regret or even renounce their earlier lives. It is common for poets to use language like "I had to forget everything I ever learned to make way for new work" or "You must learn all the rules so that you can break them." This is, paradoxically, clichéd thinking, a symptom of our fragmented existences rather than a useful ingenuousness or regenerative naïveté. Art – including our own, perhaps especially our own – should help us to integrate existence rather than mark it off. We should learn to see our lives as one time rather than a series of separate times. I find it difficult to believe in radical conversion stories – Saul on the road to Damascus and all that. I think you can test the truth of a man's present against his past; indeed, I think you have to. Our most transfiguring spiritual experiences are merely the experiences we were trying to have all our lives, which is to say that we are not so much transfigured as completed.

Christian Wiman is the author of two books of poetry. A collection of his prose, *Ambition And Survival: Becoming A Poet*, will appear in September. He is the editor of *Poetry*.

Some Related Reading
Dietrich Bonhoeffer, *Letters and Papers from Prison*, 1953
George Lindbeck, *The Nature of Doctrine*, 1984
Jürgen Moltmann, *The Crucified God*, 1972
Marilynne Robinson, *Housekeeping,* 1980; *Gilead*, 2005
Paul Tillich, *The Courage to Be*, 1952
Miguel de Unamuno, *Tragic Sense of Life*, 1913

Is Performance Poetry Dead?

CORNELIA GRÄBNER

In 2006, *Poetry International* at London's South Bank Centre included a debate between performance poets Lemn Sissay and Luke Wright. As one of the two or three people who voted for Lemn Sissay's contention that performance poetry is dead, I would like to continue this – in my opinion, long overdue – debate from my own perspective, as an academic specialising in performance poetry.

Crucial to our question is what we mean by 'performance poetry'. From arguments made on the day, I deduce that *Luke Wright* defines it as poetry that mobilizes not a reading but a speaking voice, and which puts the word in contact with music, non-musical sounds, visual elements and theatrical devices. These elements are not usually mobilized by 'written' or 'recited' poetry and therefore are not traditionally considered 'poetic'. However, in performance poetry they function as part of the poem because they are indispensable to the *meaning production* of the poem. From this perspective performance poetry is indeed alive and well: many poets mobilize such elements.

Lemn Sissay made the counter-argument that performance poetry is dead because the showing element has received so much emphasis that it drowns out the *actual work with words*.[1] He was especially critical of Slam poetry which proposes a notion of competition he sees as adverse to art. Sissay argues that an artist is not competing for the approval of the audience, but that s/he is always in competition with her- or himself. Performance poetry, having mutated into a show, is dead. According to these arguments Wright considers the main characteristic of performance poetry to be the performance itself. Sissay considers performance poetry to be poetry first of all; and performance to be a subordinate characteristic.

I'd like to introduce another – provocative – argument into this discussion by extending Wright's primarily *style*-oriented definition of performance poetry. I agree with him that performance poetry is characterized by its mobilization of poetic devices which are not elements of written poetry. However, my argument is that the mobilization of these devices is bound up with the *content* of performance poetry.

Let me take a short detour through the history of performance poetry. From the 1950s to the 1970s, poetry *performance* – especially in English –

---

1. Lemn Sissay outlines this argument in his 'News from the Beat' in *PR 96:4* pp. 122–3 (- Ed.)

developed mainly as a form of protest and rebellion: think of the Beat Poets. At the same time other poets, such as Langston Hughes,[2] developed the practice as cultural expression. Because it worked well in both contexts, it was quickly adopted by artists committed to particular social and political movements. Poets like Amiri Baraka, Gil Scott Heron, The Last Poets and Linton Kwesi Johnson made concrete demands for social and political change. (This differentiated them from most of the Beat Poets.) They took a step beyond complaint, addressing their audiences as a community with whom they shared experiences, values and convictions. In these communities, the availability of the poet for discussion and interaction with his/her audience questioned authoritarian power relations that worked not only in the political, but also in the cultural field; the poet was now *situated within* his community, not someone who was superior to it because of sophisticated expression or depth of thought. Furthermore, the mobilization of sonic, visual and theatrical devices allowed poets to emphasize speech rhythm, vernaculars, and the cultural connotations of music. Poetry performance allowed the poets to *perform* a cultural identity that was a political issue, linked with concrete political demands.

As Amiri Baraka explains:

> We had evolved through our practice a growing rationale for what we felt and did. We wanted Black Art. We felt it could move our people, the Afro American people, to revolutionary positions [...]. We wanted Black Art that was 1. *Identifiably Afro American*. As Black as Bessie Smith or Billie Holiday or Duke Ellington or John Coltrane. That is, we wanted it to express our lives and history, our needs and desires. Our will and our passion. Our self determination, self respect and self defense. 2. We wanted it to be a *Mass Art*. We wanted it to Boogaloo (like them Deacons for Self Defense down in Boogaloosa, La., when they routed the Klan). Yeh, Boogaloo out the class rooms and elitist dens of iniquitous obliquity and speak and sing and scream abroad among Black people! We wanted a mass popular art, distinct from the tedious abstractions our oppressors and their negroes bamboozled the "few" as Art. (Baraka 2000: 502)

In 1996, Linton Kwesi Johnson is articulating a similar attitude:

---

2. The case of Hughes – whose work started in the 1920s – shows clearly how the articulation and performance of an oppressed cultural identity can be an expression of rebellion.

> [...] my initial impetus to write had nothing to do with a feel
> for poetry or a grounding in poetry, rather it was an urgency
> to express the anger and the frustrations and the hopes and
> the aspirations of my generation growing up in this country
> under the shadow of racism. (Caesar: 62)

In the same interview Johnson goes on to explain how he started working with percussion, voice, and reggae because he felt that poetic language, filtered through them, better expressed his everyday experience. As these examples demonstrate, sonic, visual, theatrical and social devices were not introduced because poets thought they would be entertaining or valuable *in themselves*, but in order to validate specific poetic and cultural traditions which provided poets with both the foundation and means to express their political visions and demands.

One might counter this argument by saying that all poetry – not only political work – is originally oral; and that therefore I should not 'appropriate' stylistic devices to purely political performance poetry. I agree that poetry was originally oral. However, I would suggest that this tradition had almost died out in the dominant cultures of the North Atlantic region until oral traditions from other cultures resuscitated it. Where white performance poets responded to the revival of orality, they often did so from an equally politically committed position. Therefore, my argument remains valid: the performance of poetry as we know it today is historically bound up with the consciousness of the poet's position within his social and political surroundings, and with political demands that are the results of her/his position or self-positioning.[3]

Before I return to my analysis of Wright's and Sissay's arguments I want to go somewhat deeper into the definition of poetry performance. Luke Wright suggests that performance is a value in itself; Lemn Sissay argues that it is not. In fact, he is critical of the term performance, which he associates with a pretence or show. However, 'performance' can mean different things. In *Performance Studies: An Introduction*, Richard Schechner argues that performance can be related to *being, doing,* and *showing doing* (Schechner 2002). In the context of poetry performance the last of these is the most interesting. When a performer is "showing doing" in relation to social and cultural roles, then s/he stages, i.e. makes obvious, the patterns that inform our performance of social and cultural roles. Moreover, according to Henry

---

3. I differentiate between the poetry reading and performance poetry. My argument is that the poetry reading mobilizes the voice of the poet primarily as a reading, not as a speaking, voice. Also, it does not mobilize the sonic, theatrical and musical elements characteristic of poetry performance.

Sayre, performance can also, fourthly, be *an enactment* of a *previously written* text (Sayre 1995). One can take Sayre literally and argue that he is referring to a written text, or one can read his statement metaphorically and apply it to a prescripted social role. In both cases, there is a risk that performance can become pretence.

Sissay's own 'performance' at the *Poetry International* debate was an excellent example of "showing doing". His seemingly chaotic 'recital' of two poems – which was accompanied by interspaced comments, stuttering, apparent indecision about which poem to recite, breaking off a poem after a few lines because he did not like the way he was reciting it, and other 'failures' – was in fact *a performance of the poetry performance*: an attempt to show what goes on in the poet when he has to perform, and to deconstruct his own authority as a poet while claiming, instead, that of a human being. Sissay's performance raised questions about the audience's expectations from the poet, about the poet's way of relating himself to the audience, and about the role that poetic language plays as a medium between the two.

The performance as an act of "showing doing" can be a powerful instrument for political struggle because it can *either* emphasize cultural practices and affirm and validate them in doing so, or stage them and, in doing so, question them. My contention is that much of the controversy about *performance* poetry hinges on what different parties mean by the term performance and what they want to use it for: as a show – or as a tool for the interrogation of social norms and/or the affirmation of cultural practices. Unfortunately the issue is hardly ever directly addressed because, I suggest, (re-)claiming the political dimension of traditional performance poetry invests the art form and its practitioners with a moral and ethical authority that even those who have an underdeveloped political agenda or none at all would regret conceding.[4]

If we admit the political and social into our definition of performance poetry, then the practice is not quite dead yet – but is definitely on its last legs. For example, one of the poems Wright performed at *Poetry International*, a piece on the riots in the Edmonton Ikea warehouse in February 2005, used elements of Linton Kwesi Johnson's poem 'Five Nights of Bleeding'. However, this borrowing fails for two reasons. Johnson's poem cannot be separated from the context of racist and social exclusion, discrimination and police violence in which the events it describes took place. Unless Wright wants to suggest that the contemporary English middle classes are subjected to analogous oppression, the poetic analogy does not

---

4. Or because other poetic traditions bear their social and political agendas in different ways – *vide* John Kinsella, in *PR 97:1*, pp.66–79 (- Ed.)

seem justified. If he wants to suggest that such oppression exists, he needs to make the case more clearly. Moreover, the poem is disconnected from its social context: analogy with 'Five Nights of Bleeding' would entail an exploration of what it means to be white, male and middle class in contemporary Britain. The poem I heard unfolds solely in the context provided by the stage and the devices that Wright considers to be defining for performance poetry. Its disconnection from social complexities turns the poem into a display of the 'madness' of *other* people who are bargain-hunting at Ikea and accidentally cause a riot in the process. The poem becomes a show without a wider purpose.

An honest commitment to a political cause makes show impossible and entertainment highly questionable. When political causes are presented by means of show, the words used turn into an instrument of persuasion and entertainment, not of empowerment. Persuasion seeks to seduce the listener into a particular position. Whether s/he has actually thought through the reasons for taking this position is not of primary importance. Entertainment is an instrument for distraction. It does not provide, nor does it invite, a focus on issues of particular importance and often times, of complexity. Competition, a basic element of Slam poetry, is counterproductive in the context of social movements because it supplants the politically much more effective practice of solidarity.[5] For these reasons, faced with only two choices, I voted for Sissay's contention that performance poetry is dead. Given this chance to elaborate on the subject, I suggest that it might be time for poets who perform their poetry to think about whether they want to *do, display, perform a pre-written text, or show doing*; and whether they consider political demands and positions to be an inherent element of performance poetry or not.

References
Baraka, Amiri, "The Black Arts Movement." In Baraka, Amiri, *The LeRoi Jones/Amiri Baraka Reader*, edited by William J. Harris. New York: Thunder's Mouth Press, 2000, pp. 495–505.
Caesar, Burt, "Interview with Linton Kwesi Johnson." In *Critical Quarterly* 38:4, Winter 1996.
Sayre, Henry, "Performance." In Lentricchia, Frank and Thomas McLaughlin (eds.), *Critical Terms for Literary Study*. Chicago and London: The University of Chicago Press, 1995, pp. 91–104.
Schechner, Richard, *Performance Studies: An Introduction*. London and New York: Routledge, 2002.

5. I focus here on performance poetry in the English language. In Mexican performance poetry there is also a competitive practice, *Poesía jarrocha*, which is sometimes used for political purposes.

REVIEWS

❦

Don't get involved in literary organisations which are
starved of cash but richly endowed with inflated egos
and conflicting tendencies.
—*Alan Brownjohn*

Small Miracles

STEVEN MATTHEWS

Edwin Morgan, *A Books of Lives*, Carcanet, £9.95, ISBN 9781857549188

This is a loose and capacious collection, as the title suggests. The book includes civic genialities in work associated with Edwin Morgan's Scottish Laureateship alongside poems voiced by historical personae, translation, an epic of events dating back to the Big Bang and forward to 2300, a dialogue poem, sequences and lyrics amongst other possibilities. As such, and as we might expect, the quality of the work is vertiginously variable, with some very good poems inter-spliced with others more unfortunately mediocre. Ted Hughes's eccentrically myth-making approach to the post of English Laureate brought with it a mixture of the ludicrous and the resonantly powerful. Morgan's work under this title unfortunately all too often adopts the tone of his current southern peer Andrew Motion, veering between what feel like dread lessons in citizenship and governance, and decent calls for social decency which culminate in pentameter injunctions: "But let us have the decency of a society / That helps those who cannot help themselves. / It can be done; it must be done; so do it."

So ends 'Brothers and Keepers', a poem produced for a conference of social workers: hardly an audience likely to baulk at such ideals, or to sense themselves in any way confronted or affronted by the poem. What 'Brothers and Keepers' shares with the other 'lives' in the book, however, is a strategy of deploying personae to speak their "own" experiences – here to the extent of seeming to speak on behalf of the social workers:

> Oh if you ever thought we were not required,
> Workers on the very edge of despair,
> Consider Joe, kicked out by foster-carers
> At twelve, having stolen from the little they had:
> 'Ah don't know why Ah done it…'

It is impossible not to feel uneasy about such moments (and there are many such); uneasy not just because of the way the voice strays across professional and personal distinctions, but because of how trademark Morgan resistances – such as use of the urban vernacular in composed forms – seem also to have been assimilated into the brave mediocrity.

What links the various strands of the book, and what works to licence its manifold vocalisations, is a defence of poetry via its verbal and imaginative reach. Literature is the "soul" of the country; "Cosmic circumstance / Hides in nearest, most ordinary things" ('Retrieving and Renewing'):

> But better still, always far better still
> Is the sparkling articulacy of the word,
> The scrubbed round table where poet and legislator
> Are plugged into the future of the race,
> Guardians of whatever is the case.
>   ('Acknowledge the Unacknowledged Legislators!')

The shade of Wittgenstein hovers around the collection, but the scrupulousness and burnish of his "articulacy" is often absent ("plugged into" here does no real work). Whilst there is a sense of ever-renewed possibility, we are left acknowledging that there is too much talk about the possibilities of the imagination as a form of resistance, as opposed to effective rendering of imaginative realisations which would demonstrate that this is so. In a charged and pointed ending to his translation of Robert Baston's 'The Battle of Bannockburn', Morgan has that Carmelite poet conclude "If it is my sin to have left out what should be in, / Let others begin to record it, without rumour or spin". But adherence to the perplexing "ordinary", to the "record", does not guarantee "sparkle".

Which is not to deny that there are several small miracles in this book, where the words do genuinely dance on the page. 'The Welcome', "A fanfare for librarians", enacts its proclaimed virtue in a "tango of intertextuality"; several of the birthday poems for peers, particularly and sadly 'A Birthday: for I.H.F', really sail off into realms of wonder: "[...] when at last you come across the ship with eighty / Sails, oh what a sight that is to take to heart [...]" And the final sequence, 'Love and a Life', presents a heart-rending retrospect at intimacy and involvement from old age. Best of all is 'The Old Man and E.A.P.' a zesty playful allegro on the satisfactions of "springing" "tales of mystery and imagination". If this is to be Morgan's last book, a kinder editor might have worked to give such wonders a better, leaner, setting.

Steven Matthews lives and writes in Oxford.

Networks Of Panic
And Longing

DAVID MORLEY

John Burnside, *Gift Songs*, Jonathan Cape, £9, ISBN 9780224079976

"No one invents an absence," writes John Burnside. For Burnside, presence is everything: presence is invention, presence is perception. Some natural thing – a capercaillie, a meadowlark – can "centre and stake the imagination" (in Seamus Heaney's phrase); but Burnside also knows that natural selection yields unstable versions as well as subversions of life – much as a poet drafts multiple metaphors for one aspect of reality, and as most poems that are ever written must ultimately fail. The presences of nature have traditionally offered Burnside subject, theme, and even modus operandi. In this new book, those presences now also present him with adaptive forms, perceptions and language. Some of the sequential poetic forms and patternings in this book are like nothing you will have read before; while Burnside's poetic sentences fleer over line after line with an astonishing lope of syntax and skid of reference.

Unpredictability and unreliability are in fact the most natural of characteristics, in matter as well as nature, and Burnside shows as much in the conditional philosophy of many of these poems:

> Everything maps this world
> and what world there is
> is the current sum
> of all our navigation:
> networks of panic and longing,
> road maps in gorse,
> the river at twilight
> vanishing into the sway
> of cattle and bees.

There is a world's weight of being in that line break of "...is / is..." between the second and third lines. The critic Jonathan Bate argued, in the fine ecopoetic text *The Song of the Earth*, that "poets let being be by speaking it" (echoing Archibald MacLeish's assertion that a poem should not mean but be); and went on to say that "our world, our home, is not earth but language". What might we find by looking and listening to that language? What is the nature of a dwelling made of those particles called words? It can be argued that poetry is one of the crucibles, along with research science, in which language crackles and transmutes; and Burnside's work certainly crackles. The fastest evolving species is language – poetry sets temporary dwellings on its shifting edge. I believe the main aim of *Gift Songs* is to attempt get to the heart of this relentlessly fertile reality, and find consolation in its caprice.

In another life, Burnside should have been a particle physicist at CERN (the mind's destination of choice for many poets). Like particles on their trajectory from their particle-ghosts, these poems often show the 'I' travelling out from the self, or as he puts it:

> – something that comes
> from the dark
>   (not
> self or not-self)
>
> but something between the two
>   like the shimmering line
> where one form defines another
>   yet fails to end [...]

Burnside is also one of the best artists of the process of human memory I have read. His perceptual world is one where we know "what it is we are losing, moment by moment, / in how the names perpetuate the myth / of all they have replaced"; and that we can do nothing about this but watch and learn, and make language that, perhaps, collapses less easily than apparent fact and perceptible reality. John Burnside never lies to us about any of this necessarily tattery business. It is why we trust him as a poet.

Accretive and adaptable, poetry is as natural an art form as memory; and Burnside is one of our most natural and adaptable poets – accretive too; for this is his tenth book, but quite his most ambitious. Previously, his poetry appeared to evolve scrupulously, yet you could identify the species by its scrutiny of the numinous; hear it by the searching, and usually calm and calming, voice. Burnside's reliability as a poet could be "comforting" in some ways: never doctrinaire, never working with a palpable design on his readers; his close perceptions beguiled. *Gift Songs* alters any general critical perception of Burnside; it signals a dramatic change in the ecology of his poetry, maybe some quality we could liken to what he calls in one poem a "scavenger warmth / emerging from the cold". Ecopoetics could have been developed with John Burnside in mind; and the poet continues to supply wonderfully provisional answers within the ecology of his poems: provisional because his poems never pretend to an exact science; wonderful because nature is not exact either. Nor, for that matter, is language.

David Morley's *The Cambridge Introduction to Creative Writing* has just been published (CUP). His next collection of poems *The Invisible Kings* (Carcanet) is a Poetry Book Society Recommendation for next Autumn. He is Professor of Writing at Warwick University.

ℬ

Breezeblock *Auteur*

NIALL GRIFFITHS

Tony Harrison, *Collected Poems*, Viking, £30, ISBN 9780670915910;
Tony Harrison, *Collected Film Poems*, Faber, £20, ISBN 9780571234097

These two breezeblocks are published simultaneously to celebrate Harrison's seventieth birthday. The *Collected Poems* draws on four decades of work that has garnered numerous awards and global acclaim; whilst the first piece in *Collected Film Poetry*, 'Arctic Dreams', dates from 1981, and the last, 'Crossings', from 2002. Large bodies of work, then; added to which are the numerous (and, as yet, uncollected in one volume) stage plays that Harrison has put his name to, both translations/reworkings and originals. Not incredibly fecund, then, but pretty prolific nonetheless. In March of this year, Harrison received the Wilfred Owen Poetry Award, whose past winners include Seamus Heaney and Harold Pinter. So the prizes, like the poems, keep coming.

It's problematic, Harrison's poetry. Take dialect, which is both a theme and a device running throughout the *Collected Poems*, and is of a piece with Harrison's declared urge to create a "public poetry": in a recent interview, he stated that "I wanted to write poetry that people like my parents might respond to [...]. Coming from a very inarticulate family made me try to speak for those who can't express themselves". A grand aim, and one that dialect lends itself to achieving; yet strictly scanned poetry with a tight and proscriptive rhyme scheme – the quatrains and couplets of which Harrison is evidently enamoured – do a violence to the demotic in their imposition of rhythm, when surely one of the purposes of writing in the vernacular is to highlight the musicality innate in common speech. Harrison takes as an epigraph for a section of his 'The White Queen' a passage from Shelley's *A Defence of Poetry*: "The vanity of translation; it were as wise to cast a pansy into a crucible that you might discover [...] its colour and odour, as seek to transfuse from one language into another the creations of a poet." Isn't this exactly what Harrison does, time and time over? By apprehending the words of the vandal in, say, 'v.', and subjugating them to the tyranny of rhyme in order to make them kinder to a classically-educated ear, isn't the quiddity of the words – their sounds, their tastes, the manner of their delivery – being lost? Wilfully neglected, even? Not to mention elitist; look at the poem 'Cypress and Cedar': where the Phaedra reference blares intrusively, takes the empathic focus away from the dirt-poor farmhands around Harrison's writing studio and attempts to shift it to the isolation of the poet with a head full of Racine and Virgil in such company. True, there's a self-deprecatory tone and a certain self-reflexivity that alleviates the matter somewhat but an infuriating superiority creeps in: how amusing, that the football hooligan thinks Rimbaud is Greek ('v.' again).

Still, the emotional commitment and political anger can only be admired; and in that context the classicism, like that of Peter Reading, points to a (supposedly) more cultured, more dignified, age, and one which both poets keenly feel the loss of (even if that age, in a bowdlerised and diluted version, is touchable to only a select few with access to higher education; I'm not talking about wealth and breeding here, but lack of confidence and uncertainty and a need to be loved). But I don't see why a pining for an age of more sophisticated artistry needs to prove itself through wine-bibbery (see 'Social Mobility'); and whilst the technical accomplishments and mastery of delivery mostly prevent the individual poems from luring the reader down a closed alley of response, it is worth remarking that the personalisation of global events in '11 September 2001', written on that day, is emotionally and powerfully achieved without rhyme (indeed, it's the only free-verse piece in the entire collection). Traditional forms, of course, need not be anathema to the expression of political rage and disgust – but how the conscious cleverness of rhyme softens the impact, as in the opening verse of 'The Krieg Anthology':

> The Hearts and Minds Operation
>
> 'Decapitation' to win minds and hearts,
> a bombing bruited surgical, humane, 's

only partially successful when its start's
a small child's shrapnelled scalp scooped of its brains.

Those wittily-placed commas echo in their very shape the shape of the alluded-to scoop, some might feel. Can such fury be communicated via less traditional forms? Via shapes liberated from authority's imprimatur? Well, Tom Leonard does that, for one. There's very little experimentation in Harrison, either formal or typographical; despite the prevalence of italics and capitals, the page contains the words. The structure is always easily mappable. Harrison the poet loves rhyme more than he loves words, and he loves tradition more than either. His opposition to the Laureateship is sound (see 'Laureate's Block'), but the stylistics of his work declare approval of the Establishment.

When married to another, more immediate, medium, however, those same stylistics can achieve something extraordinary; and the *Collected Film Poetry* proves this throughout. Harrison's own 'Preface' is largely preoccupied with exorcising the *Blue Bird* debacle (the script of which isn't included here); but Peter Symes's lengthy 'Introduction' assesses the influence of Music Hall and WW2 film footage on Harrison's work and offers a glimpse into the poet's working methods. The work itself is strong, committed, and at times beautiful. *Black Daisies for the Bride*, a look at Alzheimer's disease, in its disintegrating and achingly evocative English recalls B.S.Johnson's great and moving novel *House Mother Normal*; and *The Blasphemer's Bouquet* is a righteous blast against all forms of fundamentalism, with its refrain of "O how I love this fleeting life!" an antidote to hate. The work within this volume is consistently compelling and stirring; almost every verse demands to be read over. It's often said that, in Harrison, we have an heir to Auden; in his film work, we undoubtedly do. But as to whether he's successful in writing a public poetry for the common man, I can't really say; this common man doesn't speak Latin.

Niall Griffiths's latest of five novels is *Rust* (Cape 2006). He has been awarded both the Arts Council of Wales and the Welsh Books Council Book of the Year (2004).

Life After Death

ADAM THORPE

Tess Gallagher, *Dear Ghosts*, Bloodaxe, £8.95, ISBN 9781852247645;
Elaine Feinstein, *Talking to the Dead*, Carcanet, £9.95 ISBN 9781857549027

If the titles of these two collections by equally-distinguished poets suggest that death is not a blank and soundproof wall, the poems within them bring us back to reality. Addresses to the dead are sent, as Elaine Feinstein puts it, "into that darkness where nothing is found"; or, in Tess Gallagher's arresting image, "the black ore of absence". The dead are, Feinstein claims, the ideal addressees in their receptive silence – which makes them "easy to love": whether love letter, confession or complaint, the poem is emboldened, not just by grief, but by the impossibility of an answer from, in Gallagher's term, "the form of your not-there".

And ghosts? Tess Gallagher elides them with birds – not like humming-birds kept in the freezer, "too beautiful to bury", but in a mind "overpowered by the idea of wings" and thus able to escape the naked fact of loss through memory. Referring to the larks' heights that were Rilke's definition of inner joy, she writes of "the soul-inside-the soul [that] resorts to bird song". In 'I Asked That A Prayer', the revenant is the mere tinkle of wind-chimes by the grave; in 'Apparition' (a retelling of an uncle's eyewitness account), it becomes a late brother's helping hand with a heavy bucket of water.

Feinstein is typically bleaker: the ghost is an obstreperous "hot presence"; a phantasmagorical if loving whisper; a "spirit [...] in a mackintosh scented with volatile esters from the lab"; or the surviving "nets of thought" in a computer. Above all, it is the invisible "you" of the poems.

Both husbands were powerful living presences. Arnold Feinstein was a chemist and immunologist of genius who died in 2002; Raymond Carver ("Ray" in Gallagher's book) one of the great American writers. Feinstein's book is more specifically "talking" to Arnold (as Gallagher's Moon Crossing Bridge talked to the dead Carver fifteen years ago); there is much love but also rancour: the dead always annoy with their cursory abandonment of ties. Gallagher's *Dear Ghosts*, – the comma imposing its silence – is much more a Buddhist-mediated meditation on loss in general; from a dead garden finch to her own breast, amputated following the cancer that stalks the book throughout. In one extraordinary poem, 'The Women of

Auschwitz', combining the death camps, the Iraq war and the loss of her hair ("breath by plover-breath") to chemotherapy forms a resilient peace-prayer. Gallagher is bewildered, like so many of her compatriots, by America's indifference to the suffering it causes: "Something silences us. / Even the scissors, yawing at / the anchor rope, can't find their sound."

Gallagher, who once claimed that "It's all right to be a little lost when reading poems", combines a natural, open voice with a liberal sweep of imagery and reference. Mostly this is very effective, clunking only when the abundant stock of affection and affirmation hits one abstract noun too many. 'Sugarcane', describing the homecoming of her (previous) pilot husband from Vietnam, is an extraordinary amalgam of sex, pain and war in which the couple's ensuing childlessness is seen as "payment / in kind for those flaming children // we took into the elsewhere". 'Fire Starter' moves further back and further forward, to "WWII" and Iraq. The poem is an out-standing lament for a time before the "open malevolence of this young / millennium"; picturing her logger-turned-pipefitter father kindling hearth-fires in neighbours' homes out of simple helpfulness, the grown-up poet now smells "the sweet wood-smoke nostalgia of democracy" as Bush trades away liberty "for general safety". The collection as a whole fills the "hope-coffers" against all the odds.

For Elaine Feinstein, grief brings a further transparency, but even those poems dated well before her husband's death refuse lyrical embellishment. At times this risks bathos ("At your bedside, I feel like someone / who has escaped too lightly / from the great hell of the camps"), or a tendency to use tired imagery ("to begin again [...] like [...] a jumpstart"), but elsewhere it leads to the crystallisation of an entire, intimate history in just a few stanzas; as in 'Folk Song', a bitter-sweet ballad relating how the poet once gave "your treasured / Alan Lomax anthologies in lieu" of unpaid rent and "Twenty years later you were still telling the story / as a bitter sign of how little I knew you". Glimpses of early happy days in a two-room flat or "setting up tent in a rainy Cornish field" punctuate a portrait of a grumpy old man who argued "with two fingers in [his] ears, / like a child", or "filled the house with clay and wire models". In 'Wheelchair', a strange contentment is found when the poet wheels her husband about abroad after he's broken his leg: "you needed an attention that I hardly ever pay / while I enjoyed the knowledge that you couldn't get away".

Loss softens the bitterness, as 'Widow's Necklace' reveals, pitting friends' and childrens' more mordant versions against the narrator's own memory of "your warm back as we slept like spoons together". 'Home' is a superb encompassing of the last weeks where, for once, love has hold of the receiver: "Darling, they brought you in like a broken bird" echoes the "*oiseau blessé*" of Aragon's famous '*Il n'y a pas d'amour heureux*', sung by Georges Brassens. These collections may be apparently melancholy, but they bear witness that, as Gallagher puts it on watching migrating geese, "It takes so long / to figure out how to live".

Adam Thorpe's *Birds With A Broken Wing* is recently published by Cape.

❦

A Local Watchfulness

JAY PARINI

Thomas Kinsella, *A Dublin Documentary*,
O'Brien Press, no price given, ISBN 08627899589;
Maurice Riordan, *The Holy Land*, Faber, £8.99, ISBN 9780571234646;
Eavan Boland, *Domestic Violence*, Carcanet, £8.95, ISBN 98781857548594

One almost tires of the Irish attachment to place, however marvellous or terrifying that place may be at times. We have come fully to understand that Irish soil is sacred, at least to the Irish, and that the local genius is usually a poet, even when writing prose. The lonely towers of Yeats and Joyce rise in the mind of every serious reader, each rooted in Irish soil. Kavanagh's Raglan Road feels like a street one has known intimately. So do Heaney's family farm in Northern Ireland or his cottage in Wicklow.

Surely there is more to Ireland than the soil, and its various escarpments, fields, and bogs? Reading this satisfying new volume, *A Dublin Documentary* by Thomas Kinsella, I was forced to conclude that the sense of place is probably as various as the authors who inhabit these places, as long as they bring with them what this poet calls "a local watchfulness", an attentiveness that leads ultimately to "a totality of response". Kinsella's so-called documentary is just that: a mélange of documents, photographs, old poems, and prose fragments that hold the bits and pieces together, creating the sought-after "totality". The language of this volume is quickened by "an awareness of the generations as they succeed each other" [26]. The whole is a sequence about fathers and sons, about families in movement, about shifting landscapes and cityscapes.

It begins, as it should, with childhood, where "Lips and tongue / wrestle the delicious / life out of you". And "delicious" is the right word, as the tang of life itself is sensed, always evanescent, transient. In these pages, "death roves our memories igniting / Love". In other words, we love what we have lost, and our words form a kind of memorial. Kinsella is almost eighty, so it's fitting that he should rummage in his own past, although he has done so fitfully over more than half a century of writing. This is a work of consolidation, drawing together fragments from the past, quilting them, making a fresh web of connections. "I remember many things of importance happening to me for the first time," the poet muses, tracing his first moments of awareness, summoning random details that stay in the mind, "the voices of the players familiar and mysterious".

Ghosts preside over these pages: for example an elderly neighbour who "lived in one of the cottages with his delicate and very pious wife". Particular streets, such as Bow Lane, emerge from the shallows of memory as the poet is "swallowed into chambery dusk". But Kinsella has hardly been a stay-at-home sort of poet; he roamed the world, living for many years in the United States, where he taught at a university in Philadelphia. He roams intellectually here, remembering (for example) how he discovered the poetry of W. H. Auden at a crucial time in his poetic evolution, and was "struck by its emotional and technical relevance". One hears Auden bleeding through Kinsella in poems such as 'Baggot Street Deserta', which opens:

> Lulled, at silence, the spent attack.
>
> The will to work is laid aside.
> The breaking-cry, the strain of the rack,
> Yield, are at peace. The window is wide
> On a crawling arch of stars, and the night
> Reacts faintly to the mathematic
> Passion of a cello suite
> Plotting the quiet of my attic.

As he notes, "Versing, like an exile, makes / A virtuoso of the heart". That is, the poet and the exile live by displacement; they sift the loamy soil of memory, surviving on the shards they find there, piecing these shards together.

I remember fondly the icy particularities of Kinsella's early volumes, such as *Another September* (1958) and *Downstream* (1962). A certain vagueness accompanied the narrative indirection of his later work, although Kinsella has never been less than compelling as a poet. This attempt to ground everything in Dublin seems shrewd as a late move, showing his readers that all along there has been this cityscape at the back of his mind, persistent, always available as a storehouse of emotions if not images.

Eavan Boland was born in Dublin, too. But she has moved, literally and imaginatively, well beyond the confines of that city, although Ireland itself has never been far from her thoughts. In *Domestic Violence*, her tenth collection, she writes from the very centre of her work. The literal site of these poems is often Ireland itself, with its heroic gestures, high rhetoric, and (sometimes pretentious) symbol-making held in abeyance, even fended off. Boland brilliantly attacks, and nullifies, this tradition in 'In Coming Days', with its title echoing an early poem by Yeats. "Soon / I will be old as the Shan Van Vocht," she writes, referring to the mythic old woman who, in the anonymous poem, represents Ireland. "Soon / I will ask to meet her on the borders of Kildare," Boland says, adding: "I will speak to her. Even though I know / she can only speak with words made by others." This is intense and powerful writing, grounded in Irish history and literature, as is 'The Nineteenth-Century Irish Poets', where Boland meditates frankly on what is left for Irish poets today: "The toxic lyric. / The poem for which there is no antidote."

Boland is, in her quiet way, as melodramatic as any of her forbears. This is always what I have liked about her, the clash of intention and manifestation. She contemplates this clash in 'The Origins of Our Native Speech', one of the finest things she has ever written. The poem opens fiercely:

> Ours was a nation of fever, or so
> we heard when we were young,
> contagion waiting for us
> at every turn, in
>
> the dwindling marsh saxifrage,
> the sedge by the lake, even
> cow parsley, even
> bog cottons.

The impossibility of expression dogs these poems, gives them an aura of sadness tinged with nobility, as in 'Atlantic – A Lost Sonnet', wherein "the old fable-makers searched hard for a word / to convey that what is gone is gone forever and / never found it".

I revelled in many of these pieces, such as 'Falling Asleep to the Sound of Rain,' which ends with an image of "Peat smoke rising from soundless kindling" and "Rain falling on leaves and iron, making no noise at all." This kind of lyric simplicity seems a fresh turn in Boland's work, and lends to the poems in this collection an open quality and directness that is appealing. This directness often occurs when Boland confronts Ireland itself. "They are making a new Ireland / at the end of our road," she writes in 'In Our Own Country', the concluding poem of the book's magnificent opening sequence, from which the book takes it title. With cool, even malicious, irony, she writes: "We are here to watch. / We are looking for new knowledge." Boland and her fellow lookers-on become "exiles in our own country". She digs in the loam of memory with greater ferocity (and dark obsession) than Kinsella, who seems unwilling or unable to displace what he finds, and to rage against the blight. She sifts through the domestic lives of her mother and ancestors, eyeing the seductions and quarrels, the regrets, the little and larger losses that mark a life. For her, legend becomes a substance "braided with the dust of everything" that has happened.

There is less anger but a quiet, almost unbearable, grief in the poems that make up *The Holy Land*. Maurice Riordan, in his third collection, refers generally to Ireland but more specifically to his father's farm in Cork. I thought incessantly of Robert Frost as I read these poems, with their fond evocations of farmhands and rural neighbours. Most vividly, Riordan summons the ghost of his father, whose physical labours underlie the pieces. Frost, too, wrote about digging and putting in the seed, about mowing and apple-picking. Riordan favours fencing and potato drilling, the topping of beets. But these activities are life itself for him, not unlike the making of poems. They constitute the work of knowing.

This is pastoral verse in the tradition of Theocritus and Virgil, which is to say that not only does the poet create an idyll, but he discovers a distance from that idyll as well. Pastoral verse is always about exile, even dispossession. The poet – by the act of writing poems in sophisticated forms that he will publish in a volume (say) in London – outdistances his father, at least in the world's narrow eyes. Riordan writes with a certain depth of regret for the distance he has travelled, even created. He makes poems for urban readers, most of whom will never have stood at a place like Colman's Glen, "Where the sloe bush straddles the stream". These lovely evocations of place seem remote in time, unreal, however intensely imagined in these pages.

The Holy Land, with its ironic echo of a sacred place that is far away and somehow unapproachable, is full of elegies, some of them exquisitely painful. 'Anniversary' is among the most luminous poems here, and I will quote it fully, as it only takes up four line:

> Twenty-three years my father has ripened in death.
> Tonight he will come to me as the young bride
> who shyly lifts the counterpane from the dream,
> lifts the light cloth and fits himself to my side.

This is strange indeed, but wonderfully so. The father "as the young bride" must fit himself into the son, must become him, in death as in life. A fuller sense of this relationship emerges in a central sequence, 'The Idylls', that lies at the heart of this collection. Most of these eighteen poems are "prose poems", a genre I have never quite understood. But I loved these blazing little fictions, which summon a lost world of Cork in the 1950s. In the rhythms of daily lives within the agricultural round, father and son emerge in tandem, their lives frozen but not in time, as life quickens on the pages, and one begins to understand how much the land meant to the people here, and how it lives in these lines.

Riordan is a master of verse forms, and he ends this collection with a lovely villanelle, 'The January Birds'. This is a risky form, of course, requiring not one but two remarkably good lines, which must bear repetition as well as transformation. The poet has to understand the form's odd rhythms, which are somewhat unnatural in English. Riordan does, however, understand these things, and produces casual, apparently effortless, effects. Like so many poems in this volume, this is an elegy, one in which the poet arrives at Nunhead Cemetery, guessing that "There must be some advantage to the light." In other words, the living have it over the dead in that they can sing, not unlike the wintry birds in this poem. They may, like the golden bird in Yeats, sing of "what is past, or passing, or to come". Or they may, like Riordan, simply record the dwindling of lives, the small losses that accumulate and become, at last, the half-lit memory of a poet who refuses to provide large answers, only large questions.

Jay Parini, a poet and novelist, is most recently the author of *The Art Of Subtraction: New And Selected Poems* (Braziller).

ℬ

Flawless Speeches

KIT FAN

Simon Armitage, *Sir Gawain and the Green Knight*,
Faber, £12.99, ISBN 9780571223275;
Sean O'Brien, *Inferno: A Verse Translation*, Picador, £15, ISBN 0330441108;
Louise Glück, *Averno*, Carcanet, £9.95, ISBN 185754837X

Since the days of Orpheus, poetry has been invested in stories of loss and return, haunted by an underworld which poets, even today, find it hard to give up on. If translation offers a form of resurrection – witness Simon Armitage's *Sir Gawain and the Green Knight* and Sean O'Brien's *Inferno* – so does re-writing; and in Louise Glück's *Averno*, one of her finest collections since *The Wild Iris* (1992), commentary on the classical underworld and lyric self-invention are inseparable.

"Nerves frozen", on horseback and after encounters with "serpents", "snarling wolves" and "wodwos", Simon Armitage's *Gawain*, midway through the tale, is "a most mournful man", "dismayed by his misdeeds" and desperate for somewhere warm to shelter on Christmas Eve. This tableau crystallizes the stark oppositions the hero moves between: Arthur's Camelot and the beheaded Green Knight's chapel, chivalry and unmediated nature. Armitage captures the humanness of Gawain's "purity" and perseverance; the knight's journey "through England's realm" is dominated by seasonal changes which, as the poet puts it in his introduction, resonate with today's awareness of climate change. In Armitage's wonderful, alliterative version of the medieval poet's landscapes, Gawain swerves under the "thick-trunked timber which trimmed the water", and finally discovers, not the green chapel he was heading for, but a "most commanding castle" with "sweeping parkland" and "shimmering oaks". As a "stranger", an intruder to this dreamy castle, Gawain, unlike the Green Knight at the story's opening, is warmly welcomed by the host.

Here as in his adaptations of Homer, Armitage has the knack of drawing us in too; and has produced a gripping adaptation of one of the most seductive Middle English poems. In the feast that follows Gawain remains anonymous, engaging in "tactful talk"; while the "courteous company" gathers around, and for the first and only time in the poem, he "speaks of his journey". When his identity is disclosed, he suddenly becomes a narrator, even a kind of translator, translating his tricky and fearful journey into a courteous speech that captures the aristocratic imagination. Like his eloquent Gawain, Armitage handles this delicate, elliptical moment of a story-within-a-story gracefully, converting the ornate conversation between the knights into something that goes to the heart of poetic language:

> Then knight spoke softly to knight, saying,
> 'Watch now, we'll witness his graceful ways,
> hear the faultless phrasing of flawless speech;
> if we listen we will learn the merits of language
> since we have in our hall a man of high honour.

If we are tempted to attribute "the faultless phrasing of flawless speech" to the art of poetry, we are simultaneously challenged by Armitage's own forceful "phrasing" to reflect on such translation as a high-risk discipline. It is as if, like Gawain, the translator is possessed by an obsessive ideal of fidelity, in his case to the anonymous poet's original poem. He seeks a "faultless phrasing" that will recreate his own journey back in time into the linguistic thickets of Gawain's world. Such fidelity is inevitably problematic, as he renders the original, angular alliteration ("*þe teccheles terms of talkying noble*") into a softer but no less dignified "flawless"ness that speaks to a contemporary sense of things.

Unlike Bernard O'Donoghue, who chose not to use Middle English alliteration in his recent translation of *Sir Gawain* (Penguin 2006), Armitage believes that "alliteration is the warp and weft of the poem". In recreating it, he renews both the vocal ferocity of the Green Knight ("if you smite me smartly I could spell out the facts") and the seductive tenderness of the lady ("Her head unhooded, but heavenly gems / were entwined in her tresses in clusters of twenty"). Balancing between the "awe-struck" and the "terror-struck", Armitage has produced a brilliantly well-tuned, if not "faultless", modern score for one of the finest surviving examples of Middle English poetry.

Armitage has spoken of his "convictions about the importance of the human voice" in the poem. "If we listen we will learn the merits of language", his knight says. Among "the merits of language", the reader might note the alliteration of "listen", "learn" and "language" which echoes the subtle *el* in "faultless" and "flawless", creating what the poet calls a "percussive patterning of words" that "serves to reinforce their meaning and to countersink them within the memory". In this brilliantly orchestrated translation, Armitage mobilizes language to forge an idiom that is contemporary yet steeped in the past. In doing so, he offers a mesmerising version of one of the most difficult yet rewarding poetic journeys in the repertoire.

While alliteration forms the backbone of Armitage's *Sir Gawain*, Sean O'Brien's translation of *Inferno* unravels Dante's interwoven *terza rima*, rendering the vernacular cantos into a vigorous, unrhymed speech steeped in the Shakespearian tradition of the iambic pentameter. Again unlike Armitage, with his lucid account of the underlying principles of his *Sir Gawain*, O'Brien in his 'Introduction' to *Inferno* gives a brief, impersonal account of the project, and quietly refuses to discuss the guiding principles of his translation. O'Brien believes that Dante possesses a "world-making coherence and world-promulgating authority" that Milton and Wordsworth, Eliot and Pound, lack; and identifies Dante's poem as "above all a demonstration of the power of poetry". If this gives a powerful status to the poet-translator, it also demands much of a translation.

"Your plain speech reminds me of the world / Where once I lived, and thus obliges me", one of the souls in Malebolge says to Dante; and in a sense O'Brien's translation speaks to us in similar plain speech ("*chiara favella*", which Ciaran Carson translated as "clear and forthright speech" in his version). This translation is charged with a ferocious directness, as when it depicts the burning Ulysses in "the ancient fire":

> Then flickering its tip this way and that
> As if it were a tongue that spoke, the flame
> Threw out a voice, which said: "When I escaped
>
> From Circe, who had held me there a year...

Here O'Brien captures one of the most fascinating moments in *Inferno*; where Dante the Italian poet, on the counsel of Virgil the Latin poet, retells the Homeric tale through the Greek poet's hero Ulysses ("the flame" that "threw out a voice"). Elsewhere, however, O'Brien's plain speech sometimes seems to come at the expense of Dante's vernacular openness and complexity ("*Di nova pena mi conven far versi*"). On the whole, his translation intensifies the structural claustrophobia of *Inferno*, even as it downplays the concrete underworldliness of the journey, Dante's colloquial and often violently surprising turns of phrase. Mandelstam talks of Dante's "measure and rhythm of walking, the footstep and its form"; O'Brien's *Inferno* moves with a heavy assurance through the land of the dead.

'You die when your spirit dies. / Otherwise, you live.' Like Virgil leading Dante into the underworld, the speaker of Louise Glück's title poem 'Averno' takes us through our assumptions about life and death in the brevity of a line-break; and from "otherwise" onwards we pause and breathe before entering Hades at *Averno* (Lago D'Averno), a crater lake ten miles west of Naples, regarded by the ancient Romans as the entrance to the underworld. Positioned in the "doorway" between earth and hell, Glück's elegiac voice in *Averno* questions the perplexing liminality of life and death, body and soul, spring and winter, childhood and adulthood, and above all, the "I" and "you"; as when a voice in 'Myth of Devotion' says, "I am alive, that means also / you are alive, because you hear me". Accompanied by an echoing solitude ("This silence is my companion now": 'Echoes'), Glück's new poems simultaneously suggest the relief of breaking into song after long silence and the terror of the self dispersing itself in the act of speaking, a vertiginous dilemma similar to that which Eliot captures towards the end of *The Waste Land*: "These fragments I have shored against my ruins". And Glück underlines Eliot's "fastidious hesitations" in her essay 'On T.S. Eliot' in *Proofs & Theories* (1994), claiming that "when the compulsion of speech is to find and say the truth... all utterance must be tormented by doubt. The capacity of such a mind for suffering has to be enormous". What Glück said of Eliot is true of herself. In 'Archaic Fragment', she speaks of "an extravagantly emotional gesture" and, in a sense, her poems read like archaic fragments, resurrecting themes and vocabularies usually seen as too "poetic" and "eternal" for contemporary lyric poetry in a way that is fastidiously self-analytical, yet sceptical of self-exposure. For Glück the "self" is mythical but can be reinvented through myth.

Speaking through the voices of Persephone, Demeter, Hades, Zeus, a retired farmer and a girl-arsonist, Glück thrives on the interplay of voices, creating an allusive symphony in which mythical and contemporary voices harmonise strangely: on a frequency where the worlds below and above converge tantalizingly. The pleasure of reading *Averno* involves resisting identification with any stable speaker, yet at the same time being open to the presence of a singular voice, which is both Glück's and anonymous. If *Averno*'s underworld is framed allusively by the rape of Persephone, it also bears witness to the Gawainian vision of seasonal return – "Winter will end, spring will return", as 'Persephone "returns" for "one of the two reasons":

either she was not dead or
she is being used
to support a fiction –

I think I can remember
being dead. Many times, in winter,
I approached Zeus. Tell me, I would ask him,
how can I endure earth?

And he would say,
In a short time you will be here again.

If we read this aloud "many times", we hear torment and relief, Persephone and Glück, "he" and "she", "you" and "I", palpably intertwined like the fictional "end" of winter and the "beginning" of spring. Here, the line-break (linked by a dash) between "fiction" and "I" not only creates a breathing space within doubt, but also opens up a territory of spokenness where the memory of "being dead", being "here" to "endure the earth" is shared by all of us who, like the "you" of the poem, "will forget everything", so that "those fields of ice will be / the meadows of Elysium."

Kit Fan has just finished his PhD thesis, *Thom Gunn and the Occasions of Poetry*, at the University of York. His poems have appeared in *Poetry Review*, *The Rialto* and *Acumen*.

ℬ

Firsts

JANE HOLLAND

Daljit Nagra, *Look We Have Coming to Dover!*
Faber, £8.99, ISBN 9780571231225;
Claire Crowther, *Stretch of Closures*, Shearsman, £8.95, ISBN 9781905700189;
Tiffany Atkinson, *Kink and Particle*, Seren, £7.99, ISBN 9781854114341

One of my favourite collections of recent years, Daljit Nagra's *Look We Have Coming to Dover!*, is marvellously fresh and exuberant, undaunted by the poetic traditions into which it dances, costumed and carnivalesque, teasing us with its motley cast of British-Asian characters and mischievous air of self-parody. It is not always possible to discern a guiding intelligence in a first collection, let alone a quantifiable and overarching theme. Nagra's debut, however, emerges as a book that boldly celebrates cultural identity, and which does so with such an infectious and irrepressible humour that it's impossible to categorise these poems as mere social commentary without looking like you've missed the joke.

Daljit Nagra, whose parents emigrated to England from the Punjab in the 1950s, is a poet in love with language, both English and Punjabi, which he speaks fluently. His poetry is littered with Punjabi words and phrases (handily glossed at the back of the book), and the pigeon-English of the newly-arrived immigrant – "*Do yoo tink is white Gud's wife yor mudder?*" – imbuing this collection with an intoxicating taste of the polyglot, inviting us to be bilingual too, to join in the dance of poems such as 'In a White Town':

> two of us alone, she'd duck at my stuttered Punjabi,
> laughing, she'd say I was a gora, I'd only be freed
> by a bride from India who would double as her saathi.

Reading the whole book in one sitting can feel like sensory overload, the rich scents and textures of his colourful tableaux are so intense:

> the pink kameez and balloon'd bottoms,
> mustard-oiled trail of hair, brocaded pink
> sandals and the smell of curry.

Returning to it more slowly reveals new layers, an erotically-charged energy in his comic love poems – "Darling is so pirouettey with us / for whirlwind married month" – and a sense of theatrical performance in some of his character studies, a voice well-suited to both page and stage: always a tricky balance to achieve. There's an intellectual ambition behind this collection too; a desire to address the difficult issues surrounding immigration, the stresses of growing up as an outsider, and the poignant mismatch between the values and aspirations of first generation British-born Asians and their parents: "O my only son, why will she not lie down / for us, to part herself, to drive out babies?"

By contrast with Nagra's festival atmosphere, Claire Crowther's poetry feels quiet and studied, with that curiously European sensibility, an understanding that poems can be deeply intimate, speaking as it were to one person only, yet broadly discursive and abstract at the same time. Her debut, *Stretch of Closures*, brings history and geography alive on its pages, hints at the supernatural in the everyday, and – like Daljit Nagra's – dips provocatively in and out of other languages, making that sense of otherness part of the integral structure of her poems.

This is endlessly-shifting language which surprises, tricks the eye and invites re-reading: "Home is rind-hard" Crowther writes in 'Foreigners in Lecce', "We look over / olive trees whose hips tilt / above October mats". Cryptic, disconnected, in love with enjambement, these poems readily suggest more than their surface meaning, as here when she describes the builders of 'Martha's New Extension':

> they have clambered through the alphabet
> of my house all my life and I've stewed
> tea so thick the spoon stands in the brew
> clear my dust out of their mouths.

Crowther's poetic vision examines the paradoxical qualities of endurance: the patience and mutability of the feminine versus the seeming durability of stone with its susceptibility to erosion, this last providing a recurring motif in poems about "soft Lecce stone": "A husband's hand / smells like tufa, warm, rough, / open to the weather" ('Against the Evidence'). Her poetry deals with female personae seen against a patriarchal backdrop – wives, daughters, lovers – yet her language and syntax are so hard-edged, she often seems to be subverting the feminine into something far from yielding, almost non-human – "My breasts // salt quartz" – or vice versa, with such marvellously-conceived lines as "They're millinery, roofs, pinned with cranes". This collection is quietly ambitious, not showy, but Claire Crowther is a poet whose confident, highly sensuous explorations of language and gender deserve to be read and recognised.

A more ostentatious first book comes from Tiffany Atkinson with her *Kink and Particle*, a Poetry Book Society Recommendation. This collection is also concerned with all things female, but seems focused on a generation reaching thirty who "sense they're nothing special". Her poetry is electric with tricks and starts, bristling with cynicism and modern ennui – "no one owns / the smoking junkyards of your hands" – or trying to shock with casual obscenities and laddish tales of "American sex [...] in noirish hotels". Like Crowther, Atkinson's language can be astonishingly rich and apposite, her imagery and use of metaphor superb; with one moving poem about scattering her grandfather's ashes, 'Paddling', where she describes her grandmother's bare feet as "pale Victoriana on the packed sand". Yet elsewhere she seems to luxuriate in the ugliness of an urban existence where "Dogs / go mental", saying grimly "I work my cigarette like pornography". Some poems are written in a truncated journalese, the staccato jolt of her line-breaks not always successful. But when they do work, as here in 'Nia, June 16', the result can be highly memorable:

> That, and a few other
> things we can count on, girl. Like
> taxes. Death. A Chardonnay hang-
> over. Heels. A damn good haircut.

Whilst this book is not as ambitious in scope as *Look We Have Coming to Dover!*, Atkinson's main theme is also identity; a conflicted female identity fraught with the potential for confusions and pluralism. She may describe herself in 'Portrait Photography' as "accidental, bookish, pushing thirty", yet many poems here are far from products of such an Austenesque sensibility. Witness, instead, the 'Sonnet to Hand-Rolled Golden Virginia' with its louche description of roll-up cigarettes as "Ritual origami for the spiritually lost", or this traffic-jam on the way to a funeral in 'Nine Miles Stationary': "A girl grits her heels on the hard shoulder, / sporting an inexplicable ballgown at high noon. / She spits into her mobile's cut-throat blade, / I fucking said I fucking don't know."

Jane Holland's second collection *Boudicca & Co.* (Salt) appeared in 2006.

❧

Poetry Wars

ALAN BROWNJOHN

Peter Barry, *Poetry Wars: British Poetry of the 1970s and the Battle of Earls Court*, Salt, £16.99, ISBN 139781844712489

Nowadays, unless you speak to a few scarred survivors, you might not realise that the Poetry Society 'wars' of the 1970s ever happened. Best forgotten, then? *De mortuis*, etc.? No. Those battles were real, and depressing, and one way of reading this absorbing book is as a warning: Don't get involved in literary organisations which are starved of cash but richly endowed with inflated egos and conflicting tendencies. Old issues and obstreperous personalities can surface in any generation, and devour a lot of time.

Peter Barry, who himself saw a little of the action, sides with the 1970s modernists, offering a fastidiously researched and reasonably fair account of what happened – coming from that side of the lines, anyway! In the mid-1960s most poets believed the Society had become a backwater of traditionalist no-hopers. But in 1970, in the early days of Arts Council grant aid (money concentrates the minds of factions wonderfully), two parallel movements were discernible. One was an effort by those Barry unsuitably labels as "conservatives" to drag the Society into the broad mainstream of modern verse, the other a campaign by modernists "radicals" to swing it towards late avant-garde poetry.

Few on either side could be proud of their part in the ferocious struggles that developed. Barry's theme is the success of the radicals in achieving control of the Society, its spacious but crumbling Earls Court premises, its poetry events, and its publications – notably *Poetry Review* under the controversial editorship of Eric Mottram. He maintains that a "British Poetry Revival" took place, though average readers of poetry would recognise few of the names and empathise with little of the verse. He then describes the counter-attacks by poetry "Reform" and "Action" Groups, and an eventual walk-out and boycott by the radicals. That ended three years of bitter conflict sometimes coming close to physical violence. Society staff carried police phone numbers to General Meetings, just in case.

Much trouble (as Barry explicity and implicitly confirms) was due to the radicals' refusal to consider *any* mainstream poetry worth their attention. The doctrinal obstinacy of the charismatic sound poet Bob Cobbing and the erudite theorist Eric Mottram (the radicals' principal guru) did their cause few favours; exciting talents in the experimental tradition lost out in the confrontational atmosphere. Chaos and aggression prevailed in the premises and at Society meetings, spilling over into the radicals' favourite bar next door; whose proprietor would be genuinely surprised to see this reviewer occasionally daring to take a drink.

Peter Barry concedes that the radicals committed crucial tactical errors. Mottram declined to expound his editorial policy in the magazine; refused to include any reviewing. Unsympathetic groups were purged from the premises in what felt like a ruthless take-over; the radicals were dissenters who themselves stifled dissent. Their refusal to work through any kind of "establishment" channel, and their resolute hostility towards the Arts

Council (though they may have been perceived as impatient and sometimes cynical, they *were* the funding authority and never actually withdrew any grant) were profoundly self-defeating.

The author's account of Mottram and his mission explains a lot about an impressive but determinedly difficult individual. Elucidatory editorials in *Poetry Review* about the kind of poetry he and his followers promoted – as in one admirable chapter here – would have won friends. Instead, the radicals preferred to make enemies and be paranoid about the establishment. Altogether it was a sorry period. It can only be hoped that Peter Barry is right in believing that modernist poetry now has its fair chance; and presumably doesn't need to storm frail citadels like the Poetry Society.

Alan Brownjohn's latest volume is *Collected Poems* (Enitharmon 2006).

℘

Written On The Body

TIM LIARDET

Bill Manhire, *Lifted*, Carcanet, £9.95, ISBN 1857548949;
Michael Schmidt, *The Resurrection of the Body*, Smith/Doorstop,
£8.95, ISBN 978190238269;
John Agard, *We Brits*, Bloodaxe, £7.95, ISBN 1852247339

The first thing that strikes the reader of the forty poems which make up Bill Manhire's *Lifted* is the absence of verbal clutter. I was struck by the clean diction, which makes every phrase and word ring like a cleanly-hit note. More remarkable is that this is sustained throughout the book. Manhire has a simplicity of utterance which draws vision out of the unassuming; as he does with economy of means in 'Kevin', the final poem of *Lifted*: "They lift us. Eventually we all shall go / into the dark furniture of the radio."

Death is never far from earshot, and whenever it intrudes it does so *almost* inaudibly, yet decisively. In 'Across Brooklyn', the narrator walks with his daughter past the street where they "still make coffins":

> Yes, I suppose we do walk a little faster.
> There is a faint noise of hammering, too.

This sort of understatement might be Manhire's benchmark; a sort of ease with euphemism, especially when incorporating attention to his own mortality. Understatement compresses many of these poems to a quiet power. His subject, perhaps, is spiritual nourishment in an antipathetic world; always counter-pointed by awareness of how – to paraphrase Borges – death incessantly curtails us. This is nowhere better achieved than in the stunning clincher of 'Mist':

> Bring heaters! Bring imagination's warmth!
> The date stamp makes a watermark. And oh, little Julie,
> still on the issue desk, kissing each page goodbye.

Manhire has an excellent ear and he's not afraid to honour the Keatsian notion that the source of all metaphor should be something beautiful. When the human body catches his eye, though, it is invariably through its deathward character, as in *An Inspector Calls*: "I had to shoulder my way in. / The bathtub was full of the victim". *Lifted*, an exactly-wrought and at the same time expansive collection, constantly evokes death – breathing in its own purlieus, and embodied best in the figure of Manhire's late grandfather, a phrenologist whom he never met but who feels his head with ghostly hands.

A *body* is our integral physical material, but also a metonym for death. The term has probably never been so explored in a single collection as it has by Michael Schmidt's *The Resurrection of the Body*. Attach the word "resurrection" to it, and the term shifts us into an altogether more transcendent register. Whichever body Schmidt approaches there is visceral intensity, as in the title poem of the book, where miracle, wonder and psychosexuality commingle:

> That hot smooth flesh, that shit and flowers, urine
> And something else; and the haze of down on her arms
> Up to the elbows, then the quite smooth darkness,
> Substance of shadow, her flesh, so smooth, and the breathing
> Not weary or fretful now in that limp body [...]

The phrasing is striking; most impressive when suggesting ever so faintly the rubbing-together of opposites; how "haze of down" seems simultaneously to evoke both sexual alert and the electricity coming off human flesh; while the earthiness of "shit" and "urine" tugs against the intentionally archaic run of the final line. If the stress in this instant is on the spiritual, however, there is plenty concerning the want that animates the human body. 'Wanting to Think' shines a bright torch into the cellars of sexual jealousy, from which eerie messages are sent up through the body:

> He may be dead, and yet he still lies with you
> Warming his calloused hands between your thighs.
> He may still be alive, and his lips for ever
> Puckered at your nipple, above your heart.

The unashamedly Georgian diction of this poem ("He was tall, and golden, stripped to the waist [...]") places physical and spiritual love firmly together, as if they perform a dialectic. Place this coexistent range and focus alongside such virtues as the subtly musical blank verse, the cleverly subverted aureate tone, the ironised vision and the formal dexterity and you realise you have encountered a fine collection.

John Agard's poems, unlike Bill Manhire's, swing between the epistemologically light and the politically weighty; and how successful this balance seems to the reader might be a matter of personal taste. As he has always been, he's still a cruel manipulator of the single couplet. 'Queue', the opener, gives a good flavour of the sixteen formally identical poems which occupy the first eleven pages of *We Brits*:

> O please don't knock the good old English queue.
> It gives a fair turn to anonymous me and you.

What prevents such lines from descending to the status of poetic jingle is the ambiguity which regularly inhabits them. Is this an endorsement of British democracy, or an ironic sideswipe at the currents of gradualism which have plagued its political history? No answer is given, and perhaps Agard's strength is to raise such questions without milking them excessively. At his best, he is capable of shifting in a breath from the political to the warmingly aesthetic, as in the final couplet of 'Ranjitsinhji at the Crease': "his politics would not impress Gandhi. / But O his leg-glance was legendary". And, when appropriate, Agard can be authentically sombre, especially when tackling the death of Stephen Lawrence in 'Task of Spirit':

apprentice of the sky's proportions
and now you begin

the designing task of spirit –

What I most admire in *We Brits*, viewed as a whole, is the manner in which the poet can summon up wit and tact in equal measure. It is without doubt the more sombre moments, however, which truly earth Agard's wit.

Tim Liardet's *The Blood Choir* (Seren) was short-listed for the 2006 T.S.Eliot Prize.

❧

Rising To Poetry

ROGER CALDWELL

Caroline Bird, *Trouble Came to the Turnip*,
Carcanet, £9.95. ISBN 1857548876;
Sasha Dugdale, *The Estate*, Oxford Poets/Carcanet, £8.95,
ISBN 9781903039809;
Katherine Gallagher, *Circus-Apprentice*, Arc, £8.99, ISBN 9781904614029;
Claire Shaw, *Straight Ahead*, Bloodaxe, £7.95, ISBN 1852247509

Caroline Bird's first collection, *Looking Through Letterboxes*, presented us with an *enfant terrible* who was indeed all but an infant, a poet still doing her GCSEs. Four years on, her GSCEs now behind her, we have her second collection. It maybe comes too soon and certainly it is far too long: many poems read like none-too-inspired improvisations, and there is an excess of a rather routine surrealism degenerating into twee whimsies about snails playing hopscotch and lawnmowers wearing kilts. If her first collection was alarmingly precocious, the second threatens to be disappointingly juvenile. Indeed, when she uses words like "cunt", "fuck" or "piss", one has the curious impression of a child trying to shock its elders.

It is all to her credit, then, that her poetic persona displays a certain self-mockery, an admission that if she is transgressive it is primarily in the imagination:

> I could still get a tattoo on my head,
> probably not a tattoo saying 'fuck you, all of you',
> but I could probably get a tiny spider
> on my cheek or something.

Though one wearies of poems that begin in the manner of "I went looking for mermaids / in Waterloo Station", there are also a number whose panache and verbal energy redeem the collection as a whole. Bird is adept at defying our expectations, as in 'Virgin' with its reiterated phrase "If I were a virgin", ending incongruously with "no one would know my mouth tastes of peaches / and I thrash in sleep like a baboon". This surrealism is put to good use in the comic but also dark world of narrative-poems like 'Board-Rubber Duster' and 'A Seasonal Surprise for Miss Pringle'. And occasionally – though not often enough – she rises to passages of genuine poetic urgency:

> Remember,
> you had a brand new face to wear,
> your nicest face, swung the door
> like a bell to meet her, speechless, sharp as a whistle.

Sasha Dugdale's second collection, *The Estate*, is by comparison with Bird's a sustained achievement: there are poems here that startle you into respect. Frequently there is an intimacy of touch, a hushed intensity that makes one hold one's breath. The first eleven poems form a loose sequence based on the life of Pushkin. Dugdale tells us they written during a stay at the Pushkin family estate at Mikhailovskoye. However, any fear of too much literary piety is confounded by the intensity and clarity of the writing. Technically, Dugdale is not perfect – the rhymed poems in particular can be a little awkward in diction – but she makes up for this by her selfless concentration on her subject-matter. Her gaze is that of a painter's – indeed, paintings inspire a number of her poems – and the scenes she evokes are closely-observed: there is a sort of 'magical realism' at work.

There is also a curious obliquity. 'The Conscript' is about bullying and racial abuse in the army, but its ending is puzzlingly tangential:

> The cat we feed with milk from a mess tin
> Jumps up one the window, he is empty and spry

> With a whole night's mating down in the village
> And he sucks up the milk and wanders away.

There is a similar oddness of effect in 'One of Those', about a man observing two youths on the train, one with a golden chain; the man who "looks too long and looks too much" is reminded of a python he saw at the zoo as a child. And that is that, apart from the mysterious ending: the man will

> […] run a bath and let it run and run
> Whilst the boys will run the chain between them, back and forth –
> A blank repetition of their love
> Born of boredom, born of days
> Like these between the job the train the pub.

Katherine Gallagher's new book is her fourth full collection. Though there are occasional poems that might grace the pages of an anthology or magazine, there is little of the distancing intelligence that we find in Dugdale. There is also some seriously hammy writing: "What angel held us spellbound there / by the water's pelting foam?" The sequence of poems on Kandinsky also had me less than enthralled with its "drums of colour / summoning your heart". Too many of the poems never seem properly to get going; you turn the page and find, perplexed, that they have stopped. The title-poem consists of five stanzas, but only the last is memorable:

> I'm walking the high-wire, making my mark
> poised, balanced, don't look away –
> you are my gravity's other edge.

Clare Shaw's first collection lives up to its name: in its gritty *verismo* it aims to tell life as it is. The writing is direct, punchy, and certainly has an impact. The question is: how much of it rises to poetry? Occasionally we get a sense of the sound of language – "the damp clump of a boot in the gut" – but most often the writing is staccato in its effects:

> It's Saturday evening.
> The Todmorden train.
> Smaller, darker.
> The usual rain.

There is some material that is memorable here; but in the end it is more memorable for what it says than for the way it says it.

Roger Caldwell also works for TLS, PN Review, Philosophy Now and Planet.

∽

The New Readers

MERYL PUGH

Ruth Padel, *The Poem and the Journey and Sixty Poems to
Read Along the Way*, Chatto & Windus, £12.99, ISBN 9780701179731;
Joe Amato, *Industrial Poetics: Demo Tracks for a Mobile Culture*,
University of Iowa Press, ISBN 1587295016;
Michael Schmidt, *The Story of Poetry, Volume Three: from Pope to Burns*,
Weidenfeld & Nicolson, £16.99, ISBN 9780297848707

These three very different books tackle the problem of writing about poetry for a contemporary audience in widely differing manners. Ruth Padel writes to include the general reader who may be intrigued but intimidated by contemporary poetry; setting arguments about 'difficulty', 'accessibility', metaphor, rhyme and blank verse in their historical context and discussing them even-handedly and without patronising that reader. Her focus on syllables as a poem's building blocks enables a close consideration of rhythm, stress and metre, and of the role of assonance in the patterning of meaning. There is a lighter emphasis on the role of consonants. The book is organised around the eponymous metaphor of the "journey"; and the readings themselves traverse an instructive and useful variety of work by J.H. Prynne, Sujata Bhatt, John Ashbery, Czeslaw Milosz, Jean Binta Breeze, Carolyn Forché, to name but a few. Some may balk at the marketing of this book. Fiona Shaw proclaims it is "...a handbook for living!" from the front cover, suggesting it might be at home on a bookshop's Mind-Body-Spirit shelves. But why not, since Padel's aim is to welcome new readers to contemporary poetry? Above all, she offers an informed, richly detailed and un-reductive perspective on its various, knotty pleasures.

Joe Amato's book is very different, written within and for the Academia it critiques. It considers the commodification and transformation of poetry and scholarship into "the cultural and creative industries" (a phrase recently familiar in Britain). A personal narrative – working-class, Sicilian-American, an engineer, designer, poet and lecturer – enriches deliberations on the meanings of industry; interesting analogies are drawn between engineering design and poetics. The book's content and composition challenges conventions of academic writing and publication: essays – called "demo tracks" – veer from polysyllabic words to colloquialisms, and are interspersed with lists, emails, thought-bubbles.

The writing is dominated by a post-modernist sense of its assertions' provisional nature, which makes for a spirited, engaging voice. However, the resulting asides to the reader can be frustrating, rendering an argument opaque or losing it amidst the digressions. For me at least, the voice's conventional masculinity also presents an obstacle. Phrases such as "Fuck, yeah", "Big Corporate Balls" and "The Man" (indicating Those in Power) invoke Jack Black's character in *School of Rock*, a film celebrating the very clichés it mocks. Difficult, therefore, not to suspect *Industrial Poetics* remains comfortably within the traditional masculinity it inspects, particularly as any direct discussion of gender relations is fleeting. Nevertheless, this challenge to the conventions of academic poetics is intriguing and provocative.

Michael Schmidt's third volume of *The Story of Poetry*, both an anthology and a series of critical essays, places poets of the eighteenth century in their contemporary, social and literary contexts. Schmidt is a meticulous, engaged reader, writing with verve about a century that emphasised decorum and appropriate 'poetic' diction. He is unafraid to venture opinions on the success and greatness – or not – of individuals or poems, illustrating points with detailed analyses of form, tone, diction or syntax. His insistence on understanding such figures as Chatterton, Smart and Blake in a specifically eighteenth century context makes clear just how unique they were for their time; and puts nineteenth century developments (such as Wordsworth's "real language of men") into perspective. He argues convincingly for Charlotte Smith as "a key poet of the transition to Romanticism" and in discussing Robert Burns's poetic achievements, could be laying out his own poetic manifesto for "the freedom that poetry is actually about: [...] new meanings, feelings and modes of perception through language". It's an approach which renders all the poets in this anthology freshly relevant to the twenty-first century.

Meryl Pugh was short-listed for the 2005 New Writing Ventures poetry prize.

ENDPAPERS

❧

Sticks, seaweed, crosshatchings and slashes.
—*Pascale Petit*

EDITORIAL

FIONA SAMPSON

Every issue of Poetry Review must be, in several senses, an *ars poetica*. The journal's job isn't just to celebrate poetic 'art' – that numinous, perhaps flowery, concept. It's also to show-case what *PR* believes 'works'. Inevitably, this begs questions about technique, style and school.

I hope it's apparent by now that this editorship believes, with Stanley Kunitz (in his delightful, posthumous *The Wild Braid*), that "there isn't only one kind of artist in the world, one way of becoming an artist". Excellence – and its opposite – are vividly apparent in *each* of our contemporary cliques and cabals. It's with a sense of exhausted tedium, therefore, that one finds, returning from a recent trip abroad, the usual squabbles being rehearsed. One of the most vehement, and sadly characteristic, of the current batch is that over translations of the great Swede Tomas Tranströmer. In fact, it's hard even to call this one-sided affair a squabble. Robin Fulton, supported by editors who presumably regard combat as 'good copy', seems to object to both the similarities and dissimilarities between his own versions and the subtle, expressive poetry of those Robin Robertson published recently. Robertson, on the other hand, has not commented on either Fulton's behaviour or his translations.

PR finds itself with a ring-side seat for this unappealing blood-sport, since publication in these pages of some of the Robertson versions (in *96:3*) precipitated an early Fulton outburst. What really is going on here, then? Is it the usual British policing which allows each literary protagonist a single pigeon-hole? Or is the problem one of rationed publication: if our major poets deepen their practice through varieties of literary translation, might that leave less room for the specialists? Worst of all, does the excellence of someone else's work – especially if it takes another approach than my own – threaten me and mine, somehow, existentially?

PR doesn't presume to answer these questions. Fortunately, our remit allows us to bypass them and to publish, instead, reflections on the actual making of poetry. This issue celebrates the first part of an extraordinary *ars poetica* by that contemporary master of the lyric, Don Paterson. We also get to read the mind of Christian Wiman, editor of the great North American review, *Poetry*: and to consider, among other things, the political roots of performance poetry; an all-too-familiar Oedipal struggle between literary generations in Nepal and at the 1970's Poetry Society – and, as always, the tremendous range and possibilities of poetries from the UK and beyond.

LETTER FROM KATHMANDU

YUYUTSU R D SHARMA

"Spring in the Nepal Himalayas is always dusty and disease-infested," wrote a Nepali poet in his memoirs. Even now, to settle in the dusty Himalayan town of Kathmandu is a daunting experience. Instantly, as I stand beneath the city centre banyan tree popularly known as *Kavikuna*, the Poets' Corner, I get a feeling of returning to a failed nation. To come back to Kathmandu from Europe is to embrace the bleak world of a fragile polity where Rousseau has only just been born. Though the Maoists rebels have joined the interim government led by a Democratic Prime Minster, the news that hoped-for elections won't be held has come as a shattering blow. The rebels smell a royalist conspiracy. For this nation reeling under the ongoing, decade-old civil war, there seems no end to this darkness.

During my six-month European tour, the major poet Mohan Koirala passed away. When my friend Shailendra Sakar asked what he should write about in his new column in the leading daily, Annapurna Post, Mohan Koirala came to my mind. Although sometimes disliked because of his family affiliations with the ruling Congress Party, for his art for art's sake stance, and for producing rather badly-written poems influenced by poor Hindi translations of T.S. Eliot, Koirala remained a formidable figure in the history of Nepali poetry. As opposed to Bhupi Sherchan, a poet with wider public appeal, Koirala continued to lead the Congress camp in the Nepalese literary world.   After the great poet Gopal Prasad Rimal, these two poets have influenced most of the major figures in recent decades of Nepali literature.

Coming back to the streets of Kathmandu, I find a vacuum. The best of the poets have already gone: Siddhi Charan Shrestha, Bhupi Serchan, Parijat, Poshan Pandey, Basu Shashi and now Mohan Koirala. The poets of the Sixties have fallen silent; have crawled into the great snow caves of inertia. Some of them have not written a line in decades; or are writing the same poem repeatedly. It's irritating to listen to the same poem all these years from a 'major' poet. One poet, I find, wrote a Poem thirty years ago and since then he has been assiduously laboring to write a second, without much success. Another, soon-to-be declared 'major' by the blind pundits of the literary establishment, is trying to write his first poem on Himal. Oddly, he is publishing epic after epic on the subject: when we all know what he is trying to accomplish is nothing but one little poem.

Disgruntled with the dance of anarchy in literary corridors after the democratic upsurge, Shailendra Sakar plans to leave for the United States once again. Krishna Bhakta Shrestha, retired from his active literary career, has stopped visiting the Poets' Corner at New Road. Madhav Ghimere has reached an age and stature where one feels he has done the best he could. Some significant poets, like Bimal Nibha and Hari Adhikary, have started writing political columns in daily newspapers; Shyamal and Meen Bahadur Bista joined INGOs. I find myself utterly isolated, having lived for more than two decades with most of these poets and translated several.

However, as I stand beneath the Peepal Tree I know that in the past few years the best of the younger poets have appeared out of the unknown. These were faces one met first as success-seekers. But surprisingly these young people turned out to be poets of considerable merit and zeal; rough-hewn faces, tousled hair, bright dreamy eyes; *Su-sanskrit*, cultivated in native Nepalese manners and customs and lore, coming from Nepalese countryside to the city of famed dragons to become poets of national and possibly, international renown. First came a family of poets that later introduced to us this younger generation: Shrawan Mukarung, Biplov Dhakal, Momila, Shyam Rimal, Ramesh Chitiz, Gyanendra Vivash, Vishnu Rai, Bimal Bhoikaje, Prateek Dhakal, Biplov Prateek, Bhishma Uprety, Vivash Basti, Netra Atom, Vyakul Pathak, Khumnarayan Poudel, Mukul Dahal, Manarup Nepchun and others. On introduction, I found their hands folded automatically in reverence. I recalled how I had looked at the Indian poet Jayanta Mahapatra two decades ago as he had come all the way from Cuttack, Orissa, to release my poetry collection, *Hunger of our Huddled Huts* in Jaipur. "Daju," they said, "we have been reading your works all these years."

Then came Promod Snehi, Rajan Mukarung, R.M. Dangol, Anmol Mani 'Anath' Paudel, Hangyug Agyat, Chunky Shrestha, Lal Gopal Subedi, Raj Kumar Bania, Amog Kafle, Rajendra Shrestha, Padam Gautam, Khadak Sen Oli, Tanka Uprety, Prahlas Sindulee, Bimala Tumkhewa, Maya Meetu, Neelam Karki 'Niharika', Ghimere Yuvraj, Prakash Silwal, Kishu Cheetri, Rasa, Gobardhan Puja, Buddhi Sagar, Mani Lohani and Thakur Balbase. From Pokhara came Roshan Sherchan, Ramesh Shrestha, Bhupin Vyakual; from Hetauda came R.R. Chawlagain, Samba Dhakal. The list could go on and on.

Was not it bliss to be in company of these younger poets? Tired of daily routine, in the evening I visited New Road and sat beside the *chaityas* monuments as they came up with their fresh works, the first fury of their creative ventures. Mani came with his series on Kumaris: on the blank-eyed girls selling postcards of Kumaris in the Durbar Square. Snehi recited his exquisite poems exploring love's dark horizons. Kafle brought with his series on Saddam Hussain. Nepa, who began with ghazals, now writes miraculous poems of love and hunger about the brides of bare fields in a devastated landscape. Infada's rather harsh poems exercise the absurd and grotesque as found in the contemporary Nepal. Rimal's scintillating work on pan-chewing Bodhi Bikshus, the Buddhist monks and the question of 'hunger' in the new millennium, are stark, startling and stinging; Mukarung's protago-nist rocks from the fury of raging Himalayan Rivers in his indigenous Eastern hills. Sagar approaches with his old Majhis, the fishermen from remote Kalikot. Agyat's ambivalence echoes the turbulence resulting from the assault of modernism on his traditional tribal Limbu society. His experiments with narrative are noteworthy. Chetnath Dhamala brings pol-ished haikus. Tanka's rather short poems weave intricate networks of familiar Nepalese symbols. Shrestha's subtle songs of the streets of fire festivals of hunger are revealing. Bania's poems of snow and water reward the reader.

These younger poets will, in years to come, continue the legacy of opal Prasad Rimal and Bhupi Serchan, Devkota and Siddhi Charan, Basu Shashi and Parijat, Krishna Bhakta Shrestha and Shailendra Sakar; and will fill fresh pages of languages endangered by urbanization, industrialization and globalization. Nepali poetry gets richer day by day.

LETTER TO THE EDITOR

Cahal Dallat paints an engaging picture of the later stages of the group founded by Robert Greacen and led by Matthew Sweeney, as he knew it at the turn of the 90s. [...] Before Dallat arrived on the scene, the group had published two chapbook collections, *Naked Masks* (1980), edited by Greacen, Sweeney and Chris Rice, and *Chameleons* (1987), edited by Sweeney and myself. In these publications the group is variously styled 'The Pembridge Poetry Society' and 'The Pembridge Poetry Group', as if to give an appearance of formality to its sometimes ramshackle-seeming, but always deeply engaged, proceedings. *Naked Masks* gives the date of the inaugural meeting as the 17th June 1976 [...]. Other prominent early contributors were Jenny Joseph, John Heath-Stubbs, Angus Nicholson and Dermot Healy, soon to be joined by key members Aidan Murphy, Guy Carter and James Sutherland-Smith. [...] In the 80s we were joined by Maurice Riordan, Charles Boyle, Leon Cych (a founding editor of *Poetry London Newsletter*, the predecessor of *Poetry London*) and, significantly, Vicki Feaver, Michael Donaghy and Ruth Padel. [...] By this time Jo Shapcott was an important force in the group's discussions and there were more or less regular appearances from Lavinia Greenlaw, Sarah Maguire, Eva Salzman and her then rather retiring boyfriend Don Paterson. [...] Perhaps then something of the networking or promotional activity Dallat's piece suggests became more prevalent. [...] While Dallat's memories of these stages differ in detail from mine, it was good to be reminded by his piece of a significant period in all our development. [...]

TIM DOOLEY, HARROW, MIDDLESEX

PROSE SCULPTURE POEMS

In collaboration with a group of European journals led by *La Traductière*, *Poetry Review* invited some of this issue's contributors to produce a "prose sculpture poem": using only words taken, in the order in which they appear, from two consecutive pages of a book published in this century...

Tim Liardet
Winged Life

Slowly falling snow takes fright
in a corner of his mind:

Old ideas, luckless and inflated,
a device in so many pieces –

the throng, the mail-bomb, the green light
of the six-pronged snowflake.

Orhan Pamuk, *Snow*, Faber 2004, pp.305–6

Tom Lowenstein
Untitled

One reads or one listens. Disturbing,
complex ritual! Walking in the park,
talking of life, views on meaning,
reminiscences... often on walks
we are unsettled.
                              Alone and
reticent, she survived in the back room:
a strong, disturbed woman.
She preferred her inhibitions.
These restrictions were monastic.
Daring or dancing: both were prohibited.

Emma Gerstein, *Moscow Memoirs*, Harvill Press 2004, p.5

Conor O'Callaghan
The Port

We shouted,
were known
to wing
everything,
and the dark glow
several came
to believe
and told us of,
began descending.
This pretty black.

Others jammed
in the 70s,
were well-lit.
In the 90s
and shortly before
several areas
remained passable.

One civilian
evacuating the heart
stopped to call
when I passed,
asked for something,
said "You gotta talk"

– and suddenly
it happened,
the story
I am only
telling you.
I am here,
write it, do.

The 9/11 Commission Report, W.W. Norton & Co. 2004, pp.294–5

Andrea Dow
Lanugo

They grow a fine hair on their bodies,
It's called lanugo. A fine downy hair.

Her diary: the adolescent note,
an undertone. His daughter
liked to polish silver, take out boxes,
memorise old wrongs.

An illness that she has.

Always highly strung. No make up,
no small familiar objects
on the carefully made bed.

He lay in darkness.
Smell of hidden spaces.
Documents. Light fading
across the lough. He would wait there
for his daughter to come home.

Eoin McNamee, *The Ultras*, Faber & Faber 2004, pp.109–10

Jane Holland
In Mourning

There in the dark country
in the street

he clenched his mind

going back to her voice
her delicate hands

to the love
that looked right through him

piercing, undeceived.

Ursula Le Guin, *The Other Wind*, Orion 2003, p.81

Ros Barber
Round Behind The Silence

dinosaurs
reduced to the imprints of their own vertebrae
woolly mammoths big as houses matted and frozen deep
tigers shot and skinned   beheaded stags
   in drawing rooms   and restaurants
the dead pheasants   rotting for better taste
     horses   dogs and cats
(their gone warm muzzles
hoofs and clawy paws
the lit liquid of their eyes
horses bumping
dogs jumping and rolling and yelping hello
the cats' tails in the air   vanishing ahead of her along the polished corridor
chickens and their eggs   cows and their calves
the different kinds of fish   the pig sheep and lambs
the hundreds of creatures that she
had eaten over this half-lifetime

ghostly chirruping
all the birds flown across her vision
mice garrotted in traps   rats and foxes poisoned
dead on their sides with   their tongues hung out
     the one-day-long butterflies
the moths charring themselves on light-bulbs
the bluebottles swatted   burst
all the small fruit-flies which had grazed her life on uneven flight-paths

the tiny hardback beetles in roof beams
she sometimes found in her bed
and crushed between finger and thumb
the airborne germs that lived and died in her

all of them   all of them   all of them

battering the walls she couldn't see
with invisible fists and paws and hoofs
antennae and amoebic   thready stem-things
yawling and hooing   barking and squawking
snorting and mewing   mooing and braying

squealing and squeaking and humming and hissing
Hey You! We're not dead!
Don't call us dead!

Ali Smith, *Hotel World*, Penguin 2002, pp.128–9

Pascale Petit
Osprey Nests

Sticks, seaweed, crosshatchings and slashes.
Toy sailboats, doormats, discarded rubber teat holders
from milking machines, TV antennas,
hula hoops, fish nets, rubber boots,
a broken bicycle tyre – worthless
unless put to use the birds agree.
A book called *Lucille, Bringer of Joy*;
various dried carcasses, derelict clothing.
A fondness for the shiny and artificial:
the fluorescent stuffing of an Easter basket
and large green garbage bags
that fly like flags off pirate ships.
Prize to the pair at Chapin Beach
who added a naked Barbie doll to their northeast wall.
At least a half dozen elaborate tunnels.
Sheer mass, dainty perfectionism.
More tall than wide,
weighing close to a ton.
Sanctuary word aeries
built higher each passing year.
Climb up into one for the winter – they support a man.

David Gessner, *Return of the Osprey*, Ballantine Books 2001, pp.35–6

Linda Chase
Commotion

Brace yourself.
He was going back to Ohio
to take down the storm widows,
and put up the screens.

What to make of him?
A renaissance man, a bulldog
a jukebox, a bumble bee.
I dropped a coin into the slot
way before my time.

The man that got away –
stormy, emotional, bittersweet.
I dreamed my script –
the future, a solid wall.

Bob Dylan, *Chronicles: Volume One*, Pocket Books 2005, pp.48–9

Neetha Kunaratnam
(Immigrant Version)

I like work checkout.
Stumbled upon Tesco, brass taste on floor.

Big Welcome trained staff, short and corny:
Be nice to impress. Nudge tick list,
Utter prompt: help, hello, goodbye...

Script lasted hours.
Break time, I walked drunk,
Made whizz.

Bad time began to drag. Chirrup *club-card* in my sleep.
Charm snatched chats, lit up banter, but monotony

Became stabbing customers, scanning wrists,
Struggling with beer, sore back, tired legs.

Wasn't surprised discover Health and Safety complaints.
Jaded, under strip lights, air clicked symphony:
Beeping fans left me shivery.

Urge to cheery blankness began. Spaced out,
Drugs soon sapped willingness.

Quieter moments, I thinking of water,
Amble to lavatory or airport.

Professionally charming for £4.94 an hour?
Yes? I knew stick it by Saturday,

Brain dead, fit for collapsing,
TV women beam back at you.

Joanna Blythman, *Shopped: The Shocking Power of British Supermarkets*, Fourth Estate 2004, extracted in *The Ecologist*, September 2004, pp.58–9

CONTRIBUTORS

John Burnside's latest of ten collections is *Gift Songs* (2007), reviewed on pp.86–8.
Linda Chase's publications include *The Wedding Spy* (Carcanet 2001).
Ian Davidson's latest book is *Ideas of Space in Contemporary Poetry* (Palgrave Macmillan 2007).
John F. Deane's latest collection is *The Instruments of Art* (Carcanet 2005); in 2008 Dedalus will publish his translation of *Le Tourment de Dieu* ('God's Torment') by Alain Bosquet.
Greg Delanty's latest book is *Collected Poems 1986–2006* (Carcanet).
Andrea Dow's work has previously appeared in *Ten Hallam Poets* (Mews Press 2005).
Jane Duran's latest collection is *Coastal* (Enitharmon 2005).
Matthew Francis's second collection is *Dragons* (Faber 2001). He has edited the collected *W.S.Graham*.
Cornelia Gräbner works at the Department of European Languages and Culture at the University of Lancaster.
Marilyn Hacker's latest collection is *Essays on Departure* (Carcanet 2006).
Jane Holland's second collection, *Boudicca & Co.* (Salt), appeared in 2006.
Stephen Knight's *Sardines and Other Animals* (Young Picador) was published in 2004.
Lotte Kramer has published ten collections, most recently *Black over Red* (Rockingham 2005).
Neetha Kunaratnam, until recently a school-teacher in Malvern, has published in *Agenda*, *Magma* and *Haiku Scotland*.
Nick Laird's first collection, *To a Fault* (Faber 2005) was shortlisted for the

Forward Prize for first collection and won the Jerwood Aldeburgh Prize.

Tim Liardet's *The Blood Choir* (2006) was shortlisted for the T.S.Eliot Prize.

Tom Lowenstein's publications include a volume of traditional Point Hope shaman stories, *Ancient Land: Sacred Whale* (Harvill).

Claire Malroux's poems appear in Marilyn Hacker's English translation in *Edge* (Wake Forest Press, 1996). Her most recent collection is *Suspens* (2001).

Medbh McGuckian's latest book is *The Currach Requires No Harbours* (Gallery 2006).

David Morley's next collection, *The Invisible Kings*, appears this year from Carcanet and is a PBS Recommendation.

J.P.Nosbaum's *Fighting in the Captain's Tower* is published by Hawthorn Press (2002).

Conor O'Callaghan's third collection, *Fiction* (Gallery 2005) was a PBS Recommendation.

Seán Ó Ríordáin (1916–77) merged Modernism with the Irish language tradition in four seminal collections.

Ruth Padel has been shortlisted for T.S.Eliot and Whitbread Prizes. *The Poem and the Journey* is reviewed on pp.113–4.

Don Paterson's *Orpheus* appeared in 2006. *Landing Light* (2003) won the T.S.Eliot and Whitbread Prizes.

Pascale Petit's *The Huntress* (2005) was shortlisted for the T.S.Eliot Prize.

Peter Porter has the Queen's Gold Medal for Poetry. His pamphlet, *Eighteen Poems*, was reviewed in *PR 97:1*.

John Powell Ward is a former editor of *Poetry Wales* and the author of *The Clearing, Late Thoughts in March*, and *The Poetry of R. S. Thomas*.

Tomaž Šalamun, one of Central Europe's greatest living poets, has several books in English: most recently, *The Book for my Brother* (Harcourt 2005) and *Row* (Arc 2005).

Yuyutsu R.D. Sharma is a Nepalese poet, publisher and columnist for the *Himalayan Times*. His awards include a Rockefeller Foundation grant.

Jean Sprackland's third collection, *Tilt*, will be published by Cape in October 2007.

Anne Stevenson latest of eleven volumes is *Poems 1955–2005* (Bloodaxe).

Gregory Warren Wilson is a violinist and poet. *Jeopardy* is published by Enitharmon.

Christian Wiman is the author of two books of poetry. A collection of prose, *Ambition and Survival: Becoming a Poet*, will appear in September. He is the editor of *Poetry*.